OTHER VOLUMES IN THIS SERIES

THE
BEST
AMERICAN
POETRY
1996

◇　◇　◇

Adrienne Rich, Editor

David Lehman, Series Editor

SCRIBNER

SCRIBNER
1230 Avenue of the Americas
New York, NY 10020

Set in Bembo

Manufactured in the United States of America

1 3 5 7 9 10 8 6 4 2

ISBN 0-684-81455-2
ISSN 1040-5763

CONTENTS

David Lehman was born in New York City in 1948. He attended Cambridge University in England as a Kellett Fellow and went on to receive a doctorate in literature at Columbia, where he was Lionel Trilling's research assistant. He is the author of three books of poems, including *Valentine Place,* which Scribner published in 1996. His prose books include *Signs of the Times: Deconstruction and the Fall of Paul de Man* and *The Big Question.* He is the general editor of the University of Michigan Press's Poets on Poetry series and is on the core faculty of the graduate writing program at Bennington College. He also teaches at Columbia and the New School for Social Research. He divides his time between Ithaca, New York, and New York City.

FOREWORD

by David Lehman

◊　◊　◊

American poetry sometimes seems to be split down the middle. In the summer of 1995, half the crowd cheered Bill Moyers's latest TV extravaganza, *The Language of Life,* documenting a poetry festival in New Jersey that drew thousands of enthusiastic fans. The other half roared their approval when Helen Vendler ripped Moyers to shreds in the *New York Times Book Review.* "It is never a service to a complex practice to dumb it down," Vendler argued. The division between those who regard Moyers as a hero and those who cordially despise what he does seems suggestive of deeper conflicts and some larger cultural ambivalence about poetry in the United States today.

There are, on the one hand, the many signs of poetry's resurgence. Subway riders in New York like having poems by Sappho and Richard Wilbur next to the hemorrhoid ads. Three times in 1995—on New Year's Day, the Fourth of July, and Labor Day—the nation's newspaper of record devoted its entire op-ed page to poems. The Minneapolis man who invented "Magnetic Poetry" kits for crafting poems on refrigerator doors said his company is selling 40,000 of them a month. The Whitney Museum in New York mounted a major show devoted to the cultural implications of the Beat movement in poetry. Twice now in four years, the world's most lucrative and exclusive literary prize, the Nobel, has gone to a poet and part-time resident of Boston. The choice of Seamus Heaney seems to have met with universal acclaim. The poetry that matters the most to us can "touch the base of our sympathetic nature while taking in at the same time the unsympathetic reality of the world to which that nature is constantly exposed," Heaney declared in his Nobel address. Poetry has power—"the power to persuade the vulnerable part of our consciousness of its rightness in spite of the evidence of wrongness all around it."

In May of this year, I participated in a "poetry game show" held at a theater in New York City as a benefit for the Poetry Calendar, the city's free monthly guide to poetry readings and performances, listing some 350 events on average, plus workshops and broadcasts. The host was Bob Holman, the porkpie-hat wearing author of *The Collect Call of the Wild,* a maestro of the poetry slam, who explained that the judging of poems would be conducted on a scale from zero to ten, "zero for a poem that should never have been written, ten for one that causes simultaneous mutual orgasm." Five poetry organizations fielded teams. In the Dead Poets' Slam, Siobhan Reagan of the Academy of American Poets wowed the judges by donning a bikini and a hat the shape of a wedge of Swiss cheese before reciting a Stevie Smith poem about wearing an odd hat on a desert isle. In the Instant Haiku round, Jennifer Cahill of the Poetry Society of America read the haiku she made up on the spot—a poem in Japanese about the summer vacation of a snake. As quizmaster of What's That Line?, I did a slow double take when Lord Byron's recipe for a hangover ("I say—the future is a serious matter— / And so —for God's sake—hock and soda water!") was incorrectly attributed to Charles Bukowski. But I was impressed with the *Paris Review* staffer who knew that the two-line poem entitled "Their Sex Life" ("One failure on / Top of another") was written by A. R. Ammons. The entire evening furnished compelling proof that poetry as a form of intellectual entertainment can please an audience that is wider, wilder, and more vocal than the audience for poetry is generally thought to be.

On the other hand . . . it sometimes seems as if poetry has been alotted a fifteen-second spot on the philistine national consciousness. Poetry is *The Battle Hymn of the Republic* on Memorial Day, or it is a rhymed injunction to the jury of a celebrated murder case, or maybe it is something in the air of a hip dark underground café that can help sell blue jeans. I recently saw a commercial for cheap trousers in which the American slob, male of the species, defiantly says, "I have no inner child, do not read poetry, and am not politically correct." A dissertation could be written on the conception of poetry that informs this sentence.

Thrillers, too, inform us about popular conceptions and misconceptions, and so I eagerly read Michael Connelly's new novel, *The Poet,* which is what book critics call a popcorn read, very enjoyable. It's about a psychopath who specializes in killing homicide cops while making the murders look like suicides. The spurious suicide notes have one thing in common: each contains a suitably morbid phrase from the poems of Edgar Allan Poe. In addition to being diabolically clever, the killer is cruel, sadistic, and very sick. The FBI's nickname for him is "The Poet."

The Best American Poetry can help clarify some of the confusions of the moment by invoking the standards of our leading poets. Each year a different guest editor—a poet of major reputation—chooses seventy-five poems to be honored. For *The Best American Poetry 1996* we have had the benefit of Adrienne Rich's sustained attention. Ms. Rich has long had a devoted following. Her first book, *A Change of World,* was chosen by W. H. Auden for the Yale Younger Poets Series, then as now our most prestigious first-book contest, when she was still a Radcliffe undergraduate, in 1951. More than fifteen books of poems have appeared since then. The title of one of them—*The Will to Change*—announces her poetic mandate. The National Book Award, the Ruth Lilly Poetry Prize, the Lambda Book Award for lesbian poetry, and the Lenore Marshall Prize are among the prizes she has received. The poems in *Dark Fields of the Republic,* her latest book, manage the difficult feat of wedding the unyielding voice of protest to the lyric cry, whose action is no stronger than a flower.

In January 1992 I received a letter from Ms. Rich saying she felt honored that Charles Simic, the guest editor of *The Best American Poetry 1992,* had chosen a poem of hers. She took an additional moment to comment on the series, in which four volumes had appeared to date. "The quality of the work in the series thus far is very high, and the poems diverse in certain ways," she wrote, "but they don't as yet, to my sense of it, reflect the richness and range of the best American poetry." In our subsequent correspondence she wrote warmly about the resurgence of American poetry, which she elsewhere described as a "pulsing, racing convergence of tributaries—regional, ethnic, racial, social, sexual." She was especially keen on the poetry surfacing outside of mainstream journals. "I am with you wholeheartedly in your belief that a wider readership exists for poetry than is commonly assumed, and I consider *The Best American Poetry* one of the hopeful signs in recent years," she wrote me. But "for all its inclusiveness," there are "still exclusions that reflect the deep segregations of our society, the mental suburbs in which many mainstream editors do their work, the artistic ghettoes to which too many of the best poets in the United States are relocated."

As a result of our correspondence I was determined to persuade Ms. Rich to guest-edit a volume in the series. Ms. Rich agreed on condition that I would guarantee her editorial autonomy and that the decision to include or exclude any given poem would be made by her. I readily consented to this condition, which is in fact a governing condition of the series. The final say in each volume is always the guest editor's.

In her book *What Is Found There: Notebooks on Poetry and Politics* (1993), Adrienne Rich describes the "revolutionary" power of poetry. "A revolutionary poem will not tell you who or when to kill, what and when to burn, or even how to theorize," she writes. A revolutionary poem is, rather, "a wick of desire" that "may do its work in the language and images of dreams, lists, love letters, prison letters, chants, filmic jump cuts, meditations, cries of pain, documentary fragments, blues, late-night long-distance calls. It is not programmatic: it searches for words amid the jamming of unfree, free-market idiom, for images that will burn true outside the emotional theme parks." The tradition she uses as a point of departure in her own work is that of Bertolt Brecht and Pablo Neruda and Muriel Rukeyser: poetry committed to a vision of social justice or radical change; poetry dedicated to keeping the conscience of society, affirming the ideals of human community.

With unflagging energy, Adrienne Rich pursued her vision of the "richness and range of the best American poetry" when she was reading for this volume. She was especially intent on discovering work that might otherwise go undiscovered, and she considered as many magazines as she could get hold of, including all the usual suspects plus a number of publications never before represented in this series, such as *The Americas Review, Bamboo Ridge, Cream City Review, Farmer's Market, Lingo, Many Mountains Moving,* and *River City.* Leading the honor roll this year are *Poetry,* with six selections, and *Prairie Schooner,* with five; *TriQuarterly, The Southern Review, Callaloo,* and *Hanging Loose* contributed four poems apiece. Only nineteen of the poets selected for this volume have appeared in a previous edition of *The Best American Poetry.*

Publishing poetry is almost by definition a Sisyphean task, and the wonder is that the boulder pushed with such struggle up the hill does sometimes reach the apex and roll down the other side, triumphantly. Heroic efforts are routinely made. This is the right moment to acknowledge the publishing team at Scribner, who have renewed their commitment to *The Best American Poetry* in the cheerful faith that what is past is prologue. I think, too, of the tremendous vitality of literary magazines, whose editors must work overtime just to keep up with the unsolicited manuscripts that arrive each day. *Michigan Quarterly Review* receives thirty to fifty poems daily; the editors at *Agni* estimate that they consider ten thousand poems a year. One might expect that it takes a lot of running just to stay in place, yet it's still possible to come up with a fresh approach, as *Hanging Loose* has demonstrated with its outstanding coverage of writers of high school age. And I would say a word for the small presses that have contributed so strongly to the decentralization of American poetry—presses such as Coffee House and Graywolf in the Twin Cities area of Minnesota, and Sun & Moon in Los Angeles, and Copper Canyon, in Port Townsend, Washington. They do important work, as do the independent bookstores where poetry is prized out of all proportion to its commercial worth.

The Best American Poetry cannot settle all the quarrels in the poetry world. Nor is that its aim. In fact, it is possible that a given volume in this series might hang question marks over all three terms in the title: *best* (which "privileges an elite"), *American* (when "English-speaking North American" would be more nearly correct), and *poetry* (what is poetry?). *The Best American Poetry 1996* thus enters a contested site. But it does so with an olive branch in its mouth, like the dove announcing the end of the deluge to Noah. Representing women and gays and Latinos and poets outside the mainstream more amply than any previous book in the series, this is a bid not to discard canons but to add to them, to enlarge our poetic community, and to honor the many forms and motions of American poetry in our time.

Adrienne Rich was born in Baltimore, Maryland, in 1929. She graduated from Radcliffe College in 1951, the year her first book of poems was selected by W. H. Auden for the Yale Series of Younger Poets. Since then she has published more than fifteen volumes of poetry, three collections of essays, and a feminist study of motherhood. Her work has been translated into German, Spanish, Swedish, Dutch, Hebrew, Greek, Italian, and Japanese. Her books include *Snapshots of a Daughter-in-Law* (1963), *Diving into the Wreck* (1973), *The Dream of a Common Language* (1978), *Time's Power* (1989), *Collected Early Poems, 1950–1970* (1993), and *Dark Fields of the Republic* (W. W. Norton, 1995). In 1992 she received the *Los Angeles Times* Book Prize for *An Atlas of the Difficult World,* and in 1994 she was awarded a MacArthur Fellowship. *What is Found There: Notebooks on Poetry and Politics* (W. W. Norton, 1993) is her most recent critical book. Ms. Rich has lived in California since 1984.

INTRODUCTION

by Adrienne Rich

◇ ◇ ◇

Every authentic poem contributes to the labour of poetry . . . to
bring together what life has separated or violence has torn apart. .
. . Poetry can repair no loss, but it defies the space which sepa-
rates. And it does this by its continual labour of reassembling
what has been scattered.

—JOHN BERGER, "The Hour of Poetry"

[A]s long as social relations are skewed, who speaks in poetry will
never be a neutral matter.

—CHARLES BERNSTEIN, *A Poetics*

Whoever you are holding me now in hand,
Without one thing all will be useless,
I give you fair warning before you attempt me further,
I am not what you supposed, but far different.

—WALT WHITMAN, "Calamus"

Whoever you are that picks up this anthology:

These are not, by any neutral or universal standard, the best poems
written, or heard aloud, or published, in (North) America during 1995.
From the first, I pushed aside the designations "best" and "American"
(surely in the many Americas there are many poetries). This is a gath-
ering of poems that one guest editor, reading through mailboxesful of
journals that publish poetry, found especially urgent, lively, haunting,
resonant, demanding to be reread. By temperament, experience, and
life-work I've been drawn at various times over the past six decades to

various kinds of poetry and poetics, not always comparable to each other. I've also been inclined toward certain kinds of artistic motivation, certain claims for poetry. Those inclinations are without doubt reflected in the poems I chose for this book.

But also reflected in this collection—both by what's here and by what is not—are the circumstances of North America (reaching into Mexico through Roberto Tejada's "Honeycomb perfection . . .") in the century's final decade: a decade which began with the Gulf War and has witnessed accelerated social disintegration, the lived effects of an economic system out of control and antihuman at its core. Contempt for language, the evisceration of meaning from words, are cultural signs that should not surprise us. Material profit finally has no use for other values, in fact reaps benefits from social incoherence and atomization, and from the erosion of human bonds of trust—in language or anything else. And so rapid has been the coming-apart during the years of the 1990s in which these poems were being written, so stunned are so many at the violence of the dismantling (of laws, protections, opportunities, due process, mere civilities) that some of us easily forget how the history of this republic has been a double history, of *selective* and unequal arrangements regarding property, human bodies, opportunity, due process, freedom of expression, civility, and much else. What is new: the official recantation of the *idea* that democracy should be continually expanding, not contracting—an idea that made life more livable for some, more hopeful for others, caused still others to rise to their fullest stature—an appeal to the desire for a common welfare and public happiness, above the balance sheets of profit.

As I read throughout the year, I found myself asking, What does it mean for poets when so powerful an idea, prescription, vision of the future—however unrealized—is so abruptly abandoned or driven underground? Increasingly it seemed to me that it's not any single poem, or kind of poem, but the coming together of many poems, that can *reassemble what has been scattered,* can *defy the space that separates,* can offer, in Muriel Rukeyser's words, *the truths of outrage and the truths of possibility* (*The Life of Poetry.*)

In selecting these seventy-five poems (the number stipulated by the series format), I read through a great many literary and cultural journals, requested many others. Early on I sensed that the poetry I was searching for would not be confined to the well-known journals. But I read them in a spirit of hope and discovery, and was sometimes well rewarded. I also sought out many local and regional publications, as well as nonliterary periodicals that publish poems occasionally.

Let me say here what, overall, I was looking for:

I was listening, in all those pages and orderings of words, for music, for pulse and breath, for nongeneric voices.

I was looking for poems with a core (as in *corazón*). The core of a poem isn't something you extract from the poem's body and examine elsewhere; its living energies are manifest throughout, in rhythm, in language, in the arrangement of lines on the page and how this scoring translates into sound. A great many poems rang hollow and monotonous to me; at best they seemed ingenious literary devices, at worst, "publish or perish" items for a vita or an MFA dissertation—academic commodities.*

I was looking for poetry that could rouse me from fatigue, stir me from grief, poetry that was redemptive in the sense of offering a kind of deliverance or rescue of the imagination, and poetry that awoke delight—lip-to-lip, spark-to-spark, pleasure in recognition, pleasure in strangeness.

I wanted poems from 1995 that were more durable and daring than ever—not drawn from the headlines but able to resist the headlines and the shattering of morale behind them. I was looking for poems that could participate in this historical emergency, had that kind of tensility and beauty. I wasn't looking for up-to-the-minute "socially conscious" verse; I was interested in any poet's acknowledgment of the social and political loomings of this time-space—that history goes on and we are in it. How any poet might take that to heart I could not, would not, attempt to predict. (I also wanted poems good enough to eat, to crunch between the teeth, to feel their juices bursting under the tongue, unmicrowaveable poems.)

I was constantly struck by how many poems published in magazines today are personal to the point of suffocation. The columnar, anecdotal, domestic poem, often with a three-stress line, can be narrow in more than a formal sense.

I found—no surprise—that the great majority of poets published in literary magazines are white, yet relationships of race and power exist in

*David Milofsky notes that although there is "very little money involved" in publishing poems in magazines, "the stakes, even in poetry, are high, for often such things as literary fellowships, faculty appointments, tenure and promotion are based on not only the quality but the number of publications an individual can amass. The sheer volume of submissions to this literary magazine and others can attest to the fact that publication in the literary magazines is held in high esteem by many in the arts." (Editor's Page, *Colorado Review* XXII [Spring 1995]: 10–11.)

their poems most often as silence or muffled subtext if not as cliché. Given the extreme racialization of our social and imaginative life, it's a peculiar kind of alienation that presumes race and racism (always linked to power) will haunt poets of "color" only. Like riches and poverty, like anti-Semitism, whiteness and color have a mythic life that uncontrollably infiltrates poetic language even when unnamed—a legacy of poetic images drawn on racial fantasies, "frozen metaphors" as the critic Aldon Nielsen calls them. The assumptions behind "white" identity in a violently racialized society have their repercussions on poetry, on metaphor, on the civil life in which, for better or worse, oppositionally or imitatively, all art is rooted. For this racialization is more than a set of mythic ideas: it is a system of social and demographic power relations and racially inflected economic policies, and the de facto apartheid of our institutionalized literary culture reflects that system.

Most literary magazines in the United States and Canada are edited by white men (some by white women). A few of these editors clearly try to seek out and publish work that embodies the larger reaches of North American writing and experience. But they do so within a constricting foreground of "raceless" white identity, and usually in "special issues," not as regular practice.* This series itself, *Best American Poetry,* has so far been guest-edited by six white men and three white women, including myself. The major awards and support grants for poets (such as the Ruth Lilly Prize, the Kingsley Tufts Prize, the Academy of American Poets Fellowship, the Pulitzer Prize, and the National Book Critics Circle Award) are administered largely by white judges and bestowed largely on white men. Beyond the recognition involved, which can lead to other opportunities, such prizes do literally allow someone to write—they are inestimable gifts of time. Memberships in the American Academy of Arts and Letters, the American Academy of Arts and Sciences, the Chancellorships of the Academy of American Poets, all vested with the power to distribute other honors, are overwhelmingly passed on by white men to white men, in retention of collegial associations and influence. White women writers are affected by these conditions in that they may be passed over or disregarded as

*Between 1992 and 1994, under Marilyn Hacker's editorial tenure, *The Kenyon Review* became a remarkable new space for literature and criticism, refracting the light of North American writing in this decade. Hacker's energetic vision and active solicitation policy literally changed the formerly desiccated magazine. Despite vocal protests by writers, publishers, and others, she was fired by the trustees of Kenyon College, but her editorial influence was still apparent in the 1995 issues of the magazine.

women; but as white people some of us benefit, in a career sense, from this literary apartheid.

As one such woman, I know that in a more crucial, hands-on sense, no one's work benefits from an artistic climate of restrictive covenants and gated suburbs. Need I add that when in 1992 an African-American woman delivered her verse at a presidential inauguration, and another African-American woman was named Poet Laureate of the United States, these events did not vitiate the racist policies of the state or the general human desolation the state is willing to countenance? But how could they?*

Apartheid of the imagination, like other enforced social separations, becomes a blockage in the throat of poetry. It is an artistic problem, a fault line in the tradition, it derives from a devastating social reality, and it cannot be addressed as an artistic problem only. We may feel bitterly how little our poems can do in the face of seemingly out-of-control technological power and seemingly limitless corporate greed, yet it has always been true that poetry can break isolation, show us to ourselves when we are outlawed or made invisible, remind us of beauty where no beauty seems possible, remind us of kinship where all is represented as separation. Poetry, as Audre Lorde wrote long ago, is no luxury. But for our poetry—the poetries of *all* of us—to become equal to a time when so much has to be witnessed, recuperated, revalued, we as poets, we as readers, we as social beings, have large questions to ask ourselves and each other.

Career-minded poets, expending thought and energy on producing a "publishable manuscript," on marketing their wares and their reputations, as young poets are now urged (and even trained) to do, may have little time left over for thinking about the art itself, ancient and contemporary, and *why* it matters—the state of the art itself as distinct from their own poems and vitas. This shallowness of perspective shows up in reams of self-absorbed, complacent poems appearing in

---

*What can, and does, open out the field, forward the action, for many beleaguered poets and poetries, are projects bringing both literacy and poetry into local communities, workplaces, libraries, reservations, and prisons—like Laverne Zabielski's The Working-Class Kitchen in Lexington, Kentucky, June Jordan's "Poetry for the People" in the San Francisco Bay Area, the Guild Complex in Chicago, Native Women in the Arts in Toronto, inmate workshops sponsored by groups like the Pelican Bay Information Project in California or the Prison Education Fund at Boston University, and organizations like the National Writers' Voice Project, working through YMCAs around the country, the Lila Wallace–*Reader's Digest* Foundation, and the Lannan Foundation, which have assisted these and other locally run projects.

literary magazines, poems that begin "In the sepia wash of the old photograph . . ."; poems containing far too many words (computer-driven? anyway, verbally incontinent); poems without music; poems without dissonance; brittle poems of eternal boyishness; poems oozing male or female self-hatred; poems that belabor a pattern until it becomes numbing; poems with epigraphs that unfortunately say it all; poems that depend on brand names, others that depend on literary name-dropping ("I have often thought of Rilke here . . .").

Of course, such templates are not molded solely by a culture of de facto apartheid and a ruthless "market" economy; their use, surely, has to do with individual self-indulgence, passionlessness, and passivity. But they have in common the stamp of deep alienation—and obliviousness of that fact. ("Readers of this issue," says the editorial in *The Paris Review* 134, "may . . . note that a theme seems to run through much of the content—namely, one of self-destruction. This is, in fact, a coincidence.")

I was also looking for poems that didn't simply reproduce familiar versions of "difference" and "identity." I agree with Charles Bernstein, poet-critic and exponent of L*A*N*G*U*A*G*E poetry, when he remarks in *A Poetics* that "difference" too often appears in poems simply as "subject matter and . . . local color," rather than as "form and content understood as an interlocking figure—the one inaudible without the other." Indeed, there are legions of columnar poems in which the anecdote of an ethnic parent or grandparent is rehearsed in a generic voice and format, whatever the cultural setting. In this collection, poems by Carolyn Lei-Lanilau ("*Kolohe* or Communication"), Kimiko Hahn ("Possession: A Zuihitsu"), C. S. Giscombe ("All [Facts, Stories, Chance]"), and Wanda Coleman ("American Sonnet [35]") embody dialectics of "otherness" in language itself, the strange and the familiar interpenetrating.

But formal innovation alone is not what I was looking for. The most self-consciously innovative, linguistically nonlinear poetry, whatever its theory, can end up as stultifying and as disintegrative as the products of commercial mass media. It all depends. To hold up the mirror of language to a society in fracture, porous with lying and shrill with contempt for meaning, is not the same thing as creating—if only in the poem itself—another kind of space where other human and verbal relationships are possible. What Toni Morrison calls "the struggle to interpret and perform within a common language shareable imaginative worlds" surely requires keeping that language "endlessly flexible" (*Playing in the Dark*). It also requires vigilance against self-reference and solipsism.

I believe that poems are made of words and the breathing between them: that *is* the medium. I believe as well that poetry isn't language in the abstract but language as in: *I want to learn your language. You need more than one language to get by in this city. To learn a language is to earn a soul. She is teaching English as a second language. It is forbidden to use that language in this workplace. A dead language is one that is no longer spoken; it can only be read.*

We need poetry as living language, the core of every language, something that is still spoken, aloud or in the mind, muttered in secret, subversive, reaching around corners, crumpled into a pocket, performed to a community, read aloud to the dying, recited by heart, scratched or sprayed on a wall. *That* kind of language.

Formal innovation always challenges us to "keep the language flexible." It may—or it may not—collaborate (against its own theories) with the rhetoric of deception that seeks to rob language of meaning. I go on searching for poetic means that may help us meet the present crisis of evacuation of meaning.*

I did not plan for this anthology to open with a poem by a maximum-security prison inmate, nor for that poem to be followed by a death-row meditation from a poet "outside." The alphabetical ordering of poets, a convention of this series, creates a structure of its own. I selected the poems, agonizing over some decisions, then organized them alphabetically and saw, for the first time, this book. It doesn't seem strange to me that within this arrangement I discern crisscrossings of voices, dialogues between, arguments among, dissimilar poets, and I believe you, as readers, will overhear such murmurings as well.

Until I read them in their sequence here, I had not expected what kindred sparks might fly up from Naomi Shihab Nye's "The Small Vases from Hebron," Alicia Ostriker's "The Eighth and Thirteenth," and Raymond Patterson's "Harlem Suite." How Reynolds Price's "Twenty-One Years," Angela Shaw's "Crepuscule," Reginald Shepherd's "Skin Trade," and Deborah Stein's "heat" would hold erotic colloquy from differing styles, sexual orientations, generations (Stein is one

*For this, I've looked in recent years to poets like Dionne Brand, Kamau Brathwaite, Marilyn Chin, Wanda Coleman, Victor Hernandez Cruz, Tory Dent, Joy Harjo, Lynda Hull (d. 1994), June Jordan, Medbh McGuckian, Patricia Smith, and others—poetry that flickers and articulates all around the edge of a common language, yet whose core of heat is right there between poetic and political urgencies. A poetry of embodiment more than pronouncement, resistance that can't be severed from its medium.

of three poets of high school age represented in this book). How Marie Annharte Baker's "Porkskin Panorama," Susan Wheeler's "Run on a Warehouse," and Ramón García's "Salmo: Para El" would conspire in seriously hilarious wordplay, each doing a send-up of a culture from within. I could not have foreseen how W. S. Merwin's "Lament for the Makers," in its deliberately awkward music, mourning dead poets and his own youth in poetry, would be answered aslant in Jane Miller's bitterly tender "Far Away," and, in a sense, by the vital spark in every poem in this book. How the figure of the pariah would recur—notably in Chase Twichell's "Aisle of Dogs," Martín Espada's "Rednecks," Henry Hart's "The Prisoner of Camau," Alma Luz Villanueva's "Crazy Courage," and Sidney Burris's "Strong's Winter."

The hunger for art in desolate conditions has always been one of Diane Wakoski's themes; it returns in "The Butcher's Apron," to be reinscribed in so dissimilar a poem as Jean Valentine's terse vignette of Mandelstam reciting poems in Stalin's prison ("Tell Me, What Is the Soul"), and by the four poems from behind the steel and concrete of United States prisons today. Robert C. Fuentes's "In This Place" is a shaped cry against conditions that would seem absolutely destructive to poetry, yet the poem is there, miracle against all odds. Also, from a women's prison, Jacqueline Dash:

> What an idiot (I said to myself
> a thousand times over) to perfect all that craft
> of description and describe only myself,
> as though I had nothing to show but my head,
> nothing better to tell than the mistake of a lifetime.

> ("Me Again")

I didn't know that Jane Kenyon, dead at forty-eight, and Stanley Kunitz, alive and celebrating at ninety, would speak dialectically to each other here: Kenyon's "Reading Aloud to My Father" concerned with letting go the flesh, Kunitz's "Touch Me" with holding on. Three other poets here are dead before their time (but today who knows what anyone's "time" is anyhow?). William Dickey's "The Arrival of the *Titanic*" summons that quintessential Western ship of death to collectivize personal mortality in the age of AIDS. James Merrill's "b o d y" places that four-letter word under a magnifying lens. And Jean Starr's "Flight" speaks from her American Indian sense of time, change, continuity, and death, moving from the runways of an abandoned airfield to the "burnt-out" stars overhead to "where Etowah Mound rises from the bottomland."

Nineteen ninety-five saw other severe losses to poetry: Essex Hemphill and Assotto Saint, dead of AIDS, and Andrew Salkey. None of these three (all Black men) was published in any of the magazines I saw during the year. And the fact is, many poets *don't* publish in magazines much, if at all, but in small-press chapbooks, cassettes and CDs, performance videos, anthologies.*

In this America where I'm writing now, suffering is diagnosed relentlessly as personal, individual, maybe familial, and at most to be "shared" with a group specific to the suffering, in the hope of "recovery." We lack a vocabulary for thinking about pain as communal and public, or as deriving from "skewed social relationships." Intimate revelations may be a kind of literary credit card today, but they don't help us out of emotional overdraft, they mostly recycle the same emotions over and over. The poems in this anthology are, in one way or another, victories, because they don't flinch at the materials and they don't stop at the personal.

Maturity in poetry, as in ordinary life, surely means taking our places in history, in accountability, in a web of responsibilities met or failed, of received and changing forms, arguments with community or tradition, a long dialogue between art and justice. It means finding our rightful, necessary voices in a greater conversation, its tones, gestures, riffs and rifts. These poems, different from each other in so many ways, ride on stubborn belief in continuity and beauty, in poetry's incalculable power to help us go on.

It's my hope that this collection will be used by teachers and students, by people doing the kind of "continuing education" work that deals with literacy as well as expressive writing; that it will be read alike by poets and by people newly discovering poetry, wherever they are.

I want to say here my gratitude to all the poets, including those who were almost included here, and to the magazine editors who first pub-

---

*See, for example, Joseph Bruchac, ed., *Returning the Gift: Poetry and Prose from the First North American Native Writers' Festival* (University of Arizona Press, 1994), or Roberta Fernandez, ed., *In Other Words: Literature by Latinas of the United States* (Arte Publico Press, 1994.)

lished this work. To David Lehman for asking me to do this, for his suggestions, and for his willingness to give the guest editor complete independence throughout. To Maggie Nelson, poet and literary detective, who found the "missing" poets wherever they could be located, and whose spirit has been so encouraging. And finally, to Steve Turner and the Santa Cruz–Monterey Bay Local of the National Writers Union, and to Sandra Laronde of Toronto's Native Women in the Arts, for their help in tracking two hard-to-find poets.

At the deadline for delivery of the manuscript two poets were still unreachable: Joseph O. Legaspi ("Visiting the *Manangs* in a Convalescent Home in Delano," from *Bamboo Ridge*) and Michael Spence ("Flag Burning," from *Chariton Review.*) It was painful to lose their fine poems, but I am glad to know about their work.

THE
BEST
AMERICAN
POETRY
1996

◇　◇　◇

The Tombs

◇ ◇ ◇

In the tombs,
where the walking dead greet each other,
empty souls intermingling,
having shallow conversations with words of
hollow meaning,

In the tombs,
buried alive,
Gestapo customs replace once human kind.
Oh! Sensitivity, why have you left my soul,
abandoning me to be with moral excellence?

In the tombs,
administrative mummies wrapped
in barbaric cloths.
Eyes, a mirror of psychopathic inclinations.
Oh! Compassion, please return!

In the tombs,
I once asked the living dead,
Why have you forsaken humankind?
He answered, "It's only a job."
In the tombs . . .

from *Extracts from Pelican Bay*

Capital Punishment

◇ ◇ ◇

I prepare the last meal
for the Indian man to be executed

but this killer doesn't want much:
baked potato, salad, tall glass of ice water.

(I am not a witness)

It's mostly the dark ones
who are forced to sit in the chair

especially when white people die.
It's true, you can look it up

and this Indian killer pushed
his fists all the way down

a white man's throat, just to win a bet
about the size of his heart.

Those Indians are always gambling.
Still, I season this last meal

with all I have. I don't have much
but I send it down the line

with the handsome guard
who has fallen in love

with the Indian killer.
I don't care who loves whom.

(I am not a witness)

I don't care if I add too much
salt or pepper to the warden's stew.

He can eat what I put in front of him.
I just cook for the boss

but I cook just right
for the Indian man to be executed.

The temperature is the thing.
I once heard a story

about a black man who was electrocuted
in that chair and lived to tell about it

before the court decided to sit him back down
an hour later and kill him all over again.

I have an extra sandwich hidden away
in the back of the refrigerator

in case this Indian killer survives
that first slow flip of the switch

and gets hungry while he waits
for the engineers to debate the flaws.

(I am not a witness)

I prepare the last meal for free
just like I signed up for the last war.

I learned how to cook
by lasting longer than any of the others.

Tonight, I'm just the last one left
after the handsome guard takes the meal away.

I turn off the kitchen lights
and sit alone in the dark

because the whole damn prison dims
when the chair is switched on.

You can watch a light bulb flicker
on a night like this

and remember it too clearly
like it was your first kiss

or the first hard kick to your groin.
It's all the same

when I am huddled down here
trying not to look at the clock

look at the clock, no, don't
look at the clock, when all of it stops

making sense: a salad, a potato
a drink of water all taste like heat.

(I am not a witness)

I want you to know I tasted a little
of that last meal before I sent it away.

It's the cook's job, to make sure
and I was sure I ate from the same plate

and ate with the same fork and spoon
that the Indian killer used later

in his cell. Maybe a little bit of me
lodged in his stomach, wedged between

his front teeth, his incisors, his molars
when he chewed down on the bit

and his body arced like modern art
curving organically, smoke rising

from his joints, wispy flames decorating
the crown of his head, the balls of his feet.

(I am not a witness)

I sit here in the dark kitchen
when they do it, meaning

when they kill him, kill
and add another definition of the word

to the dictionary. American fills
its dictionary. We write down *kill* and everybody

in the audience shouts out exactly how
they spell it, what it means to them

and all of the answers are taken down
by the pollsters and secretaries

who take care of the small details:
time of death, pulse rate, press release.

I heard a story once about some reporters
at a hanging who wanted the hood removed

from the condemned's head, so they could look
into his eyes and tell their readers

what they saw there. What did they expect?
All of the stories should be simple.

1 death + 1 death = 2 deaths.
But we throw the killers in one grave

and victims in another. We form sides
and have two separate feasts.

(I am a witness)

I prepared the last meal
for the Indian man who was executed

and have learned this: If any of us
stood for days on top of a barren hill

during an electrical storm
then lightning would eventually strike us

and we'd have no idea for which of our sins
we were reduced to headlines and ash.

from *Indiana Review*

Morning in
the Burned House

◇ ◇ ◇

In the burned house I am eating breakfast.
You understand: there is no house, there is no breakfast,
yet here I am.

The spoon which was melted scrapes against
the bowl which was melted also.
No one else is around.

Where have they gone to, brother and sister,
mother and father? Off along the shore,
perhaps. Their clothes are still on the hangers,

their dishes piled beside the sink,
which is beside the woodstove
with its grate and sooty kettle,

every detail clear,
tin cup and rippled mirror.
The day is bright and songless,

the lake is blue, the forest watchful.
In the east a bank of cloud
rises up silently like dark bread.

I can see the swirls in the oilcloth,
I can see the flaws in the glass,
those flares where the sun hits them.

I can't see my own arms and legs
or know if this is a trap or blessing,
finding myself back here, where everything

in this house has long been over,
kettle and mirror, spoon and bowl,
including my own body,

including the body I had then,
including the body I have now
as I sit at this morning table, alone and happy,

bare child's feet on the scorched floorboards
(I can almost see)
in my burning clothes, the thin green shorts

and grubby yellow T-shirt
holding my cindery, non-existent,
radiant flesh. Incandescent.

from *The North American Review*

THOMAS AVENA

Cancer Garden

◊ ◊ ◊

for the inauguration of the Mt. Zion Cancer Center Garden, 1995

The cancer garden, protected by buildings, one unfinished. Still
the wind will continue through the garden when these walls
are sewn in. Everything known in the cancer garden devolves
to breath. If we can, we open gray chambers and fingers
of the lung. Such breath can sting. Here are vermilion
snapdragons, mild blue agapanthus, poppy. Here in our
veins is the blood of the Madagascar periwinkle: its sulfates—
vincristine, vinblastine, *effective against neoplasm*.

In the garden we find the man whose veins collapsed nine
times, and each time the neon-colored serum stopped.
The technicians tried their tricks to open a vein,
and the strange, ambivalent poison stained (oh
how to make these poisons more selective—more
devious and therefore purposeful). In the cancer
garden we are grateful for the slenderness of needles,
the wisdom of the phlebotomist's hand. For the plain
explanation of a doctor—what is known, and what is

unknown. In the garden there is breath, ambivalence
(in the sense of unknowing—can you live with the fall
of water on your brow, drop by drop). Can you live
with the chill, with bright daubs of petal-bruised flesh,
catheter under the skin. You can look at your body
naked in a mirror, with your hands you can defend
its territories. Is the cancer sinister or blameless? Or

just cells, like all life, with a blind and blinding purpose.
An instinct to survive. In the garden, imagine cancer
as weak and depressed. If the cancer is acid, then the soil
of your body is alkaline; if alkaline, then acid. Let us
pray your body inhospitable to it. Your assertion greater
than that of the cancer—your desire to live so much the
greater. A riot of marigolds shooting up the spine—a firework

of neutrophil. In the cancer garden all the creatures are active.
Every day, a thousand kindnesses, or a thousand suspicions,
hyper-real, like the furniture of the infusion clinic. In
the cancer garden all of nature is laughing.

from *The Occident*

Porkskin Panorama

◇ ◇ ◇

I rename the continent to suit me
everyplace I stop I shop
for porkskins
I prefer the brandname
PIGGY PUFFS
make mine B.B.Q. queensize
salt intake makes me swell
at the end of the trail
see me saddleslump
over the steering wheel
I'll be a pig blimp woman
blistered skin with no insides
Jaws of Life might remove me
from the car uncrunched
next time I will travel
ballooned from the window

I prepare a dissertation
examine the phenomena
how crackly porkskin tastes
on back teeth, roof of mouth
I over-consume by two bagfuls
then drive to Porklahoma
to give the chauffeur a break
"hand over your porkskins"
I say to complete my findings

My Indian act intact: project
myself on a skin movie set
harem effects are stunning
they need a dominatrix
I volunteer for each scene
I see men crowd in halls
gabbing outside lecture rooms
they wait for women to slide
up against calico ribbon shirts
wave whiskers like catfish
that spawn the dark streams

both sexes openly discuss poetics
the demise of their lovelives
now and then men push brusquely
past women's tight ass cheeks

all vital info withheld
ouch tight marginal research
accidently words rub off
salmon jump falls for it
survive the chill of cold creeks
even a slight massage
on a rubbing ground gives thrills
to a migrating killer whale
at last someone slips the lip
some comfortable cozy phrase
strikes a pose, adopts tribal
vernacular, lets tongue loll
to recount a non-sexist adventure
in preachy graphic details

men's gossip is grandiose enough
a loud mouth woman interrupts
how she captures
authentic skin flicks
give voice to an eternal saga
last stands of lust
she pined for warriors
she mimed an ancient sign language

used by a fur trader with bald pelt
to turn handsome profit
more hang around fort
exhibitionism
occupy a backseat 50's location
but take direct action on men
with arch tendencies to do without
first nations women first
        I shoot from the lip
        arouse myself exotic
        daze myself erotic
desperate I xerox Native male poems
copy safe reproductions
because I had trouble grasping
sex ultimatums longago   teepee creepers

men don't pork dark women much
lighter ones deserve a dayglo feather
my authoritative belief
derived from meditation
upon a chief hat
the abundant plumage suggested
men counted victories
long into the night
recounted coup to each other
back at the tipi
women whooped it up
braved frontier enlightenment
the eventual decline
the multi-purpose use
of the beaver hat
even in a museum display
it doesn't speak to me
never accept an artifact
mistake it for role model
less it converses in diorama
talk created by Native writers
dialogue for duos

the light feeling inside
comes from eating a corporate volume
of porkskins for protection
still no one hits on me

I assume a dominant princess stance
to ward off advances
just where do old princesses go?
to prevent spousal abuse
I just don't score
scared my love life is unmentionable
ranked epic but unworthy of gossip
who needs beer to talk or cry?

I nightingale zoom myself
a poet's pleasure palace declare
I drive from pow wow A to XYZ
on the interstate heavy foot on gas
I even drive past heaven
never one to overpork the passions
(pass the pork rinds, please)
I start out at dawn after the dream
put on a chief hat plucked clean

I don't require a map to drive
through Billy Jack towns
each town center in the Dakotas
with white square courthouses
cries out, wants Billy back
even with a denied black hat
return appearance on a good day
to die or make a comeback

relive the Movement
how to spell relief
is sing "Release me"
from Leonard Pelletier's cell

dusk approaches as I drive into it
a dusty Rabbit City sign

next up on the distant horizon
one large rabbit mountain top
dog eaters dedicated for us
sacred Rabbit ritual territory
I find Rabid City the better name
for Black Hills tourist attractions
I ask the Native women workers
stationed at the Crazy Dog memorial
if us skins got free admission
or did the white people at the gate
make us more invisible, ignore us
we puff up with laughter
grow monumental in size
I pose for photos on a cliff edge
pork rind clenched in teeth
pantomime Princess Porkahontus

the mini outskirts of Deadwood
reckons a bureaucratic misnomer
here men stalk and sling a gun
reach then shoot out in the streets
a damn violent neighborhood
has more action where I live
the westend is badder then again
I might move to where bad guys
die in streets jump to feet
for free drinks join an arcade of dead
Indians to frequent the cloven hoof casino

I wrestle pull & jerk the slot
slut machine, word slut I become
to get the proper feel
Indian Country of the 1990's wanna bet
another winner, another gamble

from *Callaloo*

41

Strong's Winter

◇ ◇ ◇

When I hear it said of gods and great literature
that they will never die,
a cowered boy comes to mind
who carried the name Len Strong and seemed proud the day
he watched the snow fall in the schoolyard and said that God did not exist,
that he did not care whether Virgil spelled his name with an *e* or an *i*,
and now I want Len Strong to say whether the heavens and poetry
faded for him over the years, an unsleeping retreat,
or whether one night the pressing cold had pressed enough
and Len Strong woke in his winter and knew at once what he would do.

It is said of snow as it falls
that it makes the world a solitary place,
and when Len Strong broke his silence, I could not see
that a schoolyard where solitude came down from the sky
would become in this world a larger thing than God's or poetry's death.
So, under the stars above I would ask of Len Strong
that he lead me back
through the schoolyard and into the aching classroom,
that he sit in the last place I saw him
and speak of the solitude we cannot escape.

Across a snow-driven street, I would know Len Strong's lean slouch:
he walked at odds with the angles of the earth.
I would follow him through the whiteness
that grows in increments and wrecks the landscape.
It is what the living call snow, this wreckage,
and when it fell quietly from the sky one winter,
Len Strong shouldered the death of God and poetry,

which nowadays weighs little to me because of this cowered boy
who walked away and lay down one night, leaving
in my life the sharp report of a solitary schoolyard.

from *The Southern Review*

David Talamántez on the Last Day of Second Grade

◇　◇　◇

San Antonio, Texas 1988

David Talamántez, whose mother is at work, leaves his mark
    everywhere in the schoolyard,
tosses pages from a thick sheaf of lined paper high in the air one by
    one, watches them

catch on the teachers' car bumpers, drift into the chalky narrow shade
    of the water fountain.
One last batch, stapled together, he rolls tight into a makeshift horn
    through which he shouts

David! and *David, yes!* before hurling it away hard and darting across
    Barzos Street against
the light, the little sag of head and shoulders when, safe on the other
    side, he kicks a can

in the gutter and wanders toward home. David Talamántez believes
    birds are warm blooded,
the way they are quick in the air and give out long strings of
    complicated music, different

all the time, not like cats and dogs. For this he was marked down in
    Science, and for putting

his name in the wrong place, on the right with the date instead on the
    left with Science

Questions, and for not skipping a line between his heading and
    answers. The X's for wrong
things are big, much bigger than Talamántez's tiny writing. *Write larger,*
    his teacher says

in red ink across the tops of many pages. *Messy!* she says on others
    where he has erased
and started over, erased and started over. Spelling, Language
    Expression, Sentences Using

the Following Words. *Neck. I have a neck name. No!* 20's, 30's. *Think
    again!* He's good
in Art, though, makes 70 on Reading Station Artist's Corner, where
    he's traced and colored

an illustration from *Henny Penny.* A goose with red-and-white striped
    shirt, a hen in a turquoise
dress. Points off for the birds, cloud and butterfly he's drawn in
    freehand. *Not in the original*

picture! Twenty-five points off for writing nothing in the blank after
    This is my favorite scene
in the book because . . . There's a page called Rules. *Listen! Always
    working! Stay in your seat!*

Raise your hand before you speak! No fighting! Be quiet! Rules copied from
    the board, no grade,
only a huge red checkmark. Later there is a test on Rules. *Listen! Alay
    ercng! Sast in ao snet!*

Rars aone bfo your spek! No finagn! Be cayt! He gets 70 on Rules, 10 on
    Spelling. An old man
stoops to pick up a crumpled drawing of a large family crowded
    around a table, an apartment

with bars on the windows in Alazán Courts, a huge sun in one corner
    saying, *To mush noys!*
After correcting the spelling, the grade is 90. *Nice details!* And there's
    another mark, on this paper

and all the others, the one in the doorway of La Rosa Beauty Shop, the
    one that blew under
the pool table at La Tenampa, the ones older kids have wadded up like
    big spit balls, the ones run

over by cars. On every single page David Talamántez has crossed out
    the teacher's red numbers
and written in giant letters, blue ink, *Yes! David, yes!*

from *The Texas Observer*

Cauldron

◇ ◇ ◇

Gerneralissimo Yuan Shih Kai,
your horse went mad.
He danced a ribbon
around the character named "chaos."
Oh grand master,
won't you let the light in,
this human destiny,
scroll and colophon,
painterly and evocative—
is the greatest masterpiece,
dark as it is.
There are horses and chariots,
Chi'in's terra-cotta soldiers,
vengeful pale ghosts.
The men—Chivalrous and virile
behind forged armors.
The women—forebearers of sorrow
in soft cloud chignons.
The cauldron is heavy—
our bones will flavor the pottage,
our wrists will bear its signature.
As the kingdom's saga trills on,
familial and personal,
the great panorama of Loyang
blustering in silent gallows
and the war torn vermilion glow
of eternal summer.
There is my granduncle
plotting to sell my mother

for a finger of opium.
There is my grandmother
running after him, tottering
down the grassy knolls
in her bound feet
and unraveled hair.
Her cry would startle the ages.
Meanwhile, the chrysanthemum blooms
shamelessly, beautifully,
confident of a fast resolve.
Yes, all would fructify notwithstanding—
all which is beautiful must bloom,
all which blooms is beautiful.
My grandmother's cry would chill the gorges,
remembered by the caretaker of pines
in the Shaolin monastery
and the young boys taking the tonsure,
remembered by the blind sage Vitaphithaca,
his acolyte the King Monkey,
the sandman and the pusillanimous pig,
remembered by the emperor of heaven
and the yellow prince of hell.
Oh Goddess of Mercy, why have you been remiss?
I have burnt joss-sticks at your ivory feet.
I have kept the sanctity of my body
and the cleanliness of mind.
I have washed my heart of bad intentions.
And she hobbles, down past the oatgrass,
past the hollyhocks and persimmons,
orange and fragrant in their wake,
past the buffalo trough, past her lover,
whom she would not name,
past the priest and his valley of carillon,
and the red, red sorghum of her childhood.
Past the oxen and her family ox
in a rare moment without his yoke,
past the girls chattering behind the sassagrass,
and the women bathing and threshing hemp.
Past the gaffer-hatted fisherman,
and his song of the cormorant.

Oh, shoulder thy burdens old cudgel, shoulder them
in your brief moments of reprieve and splendor.
My grandmother ran, driven by the wind.
The pain in her hooves, those tender hooves,
those painful lotuses could not deter her.
As the warlord's bamboo whip flails
over the unyielding sky,
and the Japanese bayonets flash
against the ancient banyans,
history must step aside, grant her passage.

What is destiny but an angry wind—plagues and salvages,
death knocking on your neighbor's door, and you dare look out
your window, relieved that you were spared for another hour.
So gather your thoughts, brief butterfly, your waterclock dries.

Shallow river, shallow river, how shall I cross?

Footsteps so light, the fallow deer can't hear her.
Heart so heavy, the village women would sink a stone
in her name each time they cross the shoals.
The soothsayer in the watchtower espies her.
O destiny-in-a-whirlwind, serpent-in-the-grass,
she inches toward her ailing half-brother.
Dragging feudalism's gangrene legs;
their kind is wan and dying.
The child on his back, limp with exhaustion,
answers to my grandmother's call.
Night will lower its black knife,
only the lantern will bear witness now.
The bridge is crossed. My mother is saved.
Her hemp doll dragged downstream by the river.

from *The Kenyon Review*

WANDA COLEMAN

American Sonnet (35)

◇ ◇ ◇

booooooooo. spooky ripplings of icy waves. this
umpteenth time she returns—this invisible woman
long on haunting short on ectoplasm

"you're a good man, sistuh," a lover sighed solongago.
"keep your oil slick and your motor running."

wretched stained mirrors of
fractured webbings like nests of manic spiders
reflect her ruined mien (rue wiggles remorse
squiggles woe jiggles bestride her). oozy Manes-spill
out yonder spooling in night's lofty hour exudes
her gloom and spew in rankling odor of heady dour

as she strives to retrieve flesh to cloak her bones
again to thrive to keep her poisoned id alive

usta be young usta be gifted—still black

from *River City*

Me Again

◇　◇　◇

I who wanted to talk
of a time inside my soul
that is always my poem-in-progress,
have found only myself whenever I looked
and missed the real happening.
With wary good faith
I opened myself to the wind, the lockers, clothes-closets, graveyards,
the calendar months of the year,
and in every opening crevice
my face looked back at me.
The more bored I became
with my unacceptable person,
the more I returned to the theme of my person;
worst of all,
I kept painting myself to myself
in the midst of a happening.
What an idiot (I said to myself
a thousand times over) to perfect all that craft
of description and describe only myself,
as though I had nothing to show but my head,
nothing better to tell than the mistake of a lifetime.

from *In Time*

Transfer

◇　◇　◇

All the family dogs are dead.
A borrowed one, its displaced hip
at an angle to its purebred head,
bays at a siren's emergency climb
whining from the motorway.
Seven strangers now have keys
to the padlock on the gate,
where, instead of lights, a mimosa
burns its golden blurred bee-fur
to lead you to the door.

"So many leaves, too many trees"
says the gardener who weekly
salvages an ordered edge;
raking round the rusted rotary hoe
left standing where my uncle last
cranked it hard to clear a space
between the trees, peach orchard,
nectarine and plum, to prove
that he at least could move
the future's rankness to another place.

Forty years ago the house was built
to hold private unhappiness intact,
safe against mobile molecular growths
of city, developers and blacks.
Now rhubarb spurs grow wild and sour,
the mulberries, the ducks and bantams gone.
In the fishpond's sage-green soup

its fraying goldfish decompose the sun,
wax-white lilies float upon the rot.
And leaves in random piles are burning.

Townhouses circle the inheritance.
The fire station and franchised inn
keep neighborhood watch over its fate.
The municipality leers over the gate,
complains of dispossession and neglect,
dark tenants and the broken fence.
But all the highveld birds are here,
weighing their metronomic blossoms
upon the branches in the winter air.
And the exiles are returning.

from *TriQuarterly*

WILLIAM DICKEY

The Arrival of the Titanic

◇ ◇ ◇

Gashed, from her long immobility on the sea-bed
gravid with the dreams of invertebrates, only half
here in the sense of consciousness, she pulls,
grey on a grey morning, into New York Harbor,
bearing all of the dead in their attitudes, the old dead
in dinner jackets, bare feet encrusted with barnacles,
their pearl eyes, their old assurance of conquest
over the negligent elements, and walking thin and
perplexed among them the new dead who
never realized on what crossing they had embarked.

We are the photograph's negative, made after
the color print, made after the abyssal waters
took color out of the Liberty scarves, the bright
upper atmosphere of tea dances, after the drift
downward, the pressures of winter. If it has been
abandoned, it is ours, it comes sailing silently
back with us. There were never enough
lifeboats, and never
enough gaiety to see us safely through past moonrise
and our monochrome exploration into the range of ice.

from *Poetry*

A History of Navigation

◇ ◇ ◇

1. INSOMNIA

Awake at midnight on the factory side of town,
I swear the only thing I haven't tried

is counting ships. The Water Witch, the Golden Fleece,
the Silver Wake, the Sailor Boy, the Morning Star,

and last, the Kalamazoo. I made that up. This shipwrecked town—
I can almost *see* its rooftops fathoms down.

I think the starless night is trying to push
right through the walls of this house.

So is the screaming train en route through our backyard
with a load of dark that would fill up Lake Michigan.

Streetlight pours through a flowering rent
on a sheet that curtains our bedroom window;

my sleeping husband is another window
dark for hours now, and I am watching him,

too far out to care for signs and omens:
the traffic light blinks red and red and red;

the Minute Market, lit inside, shuts off.
I call it Murder Market; someone was shot there once.

How can he sleep through the dirty sound?
Garage bands never sleep. The singer's voice

is husky, dragged through mud.
Just one way to tell a love story.

Not our story, in particular,
or his. The story of an open mouth.

★

Mouth opens, breathing quietly,
you seem to skim over the water, as a ship does.
How can you sleep?
Halfway down the street, a man is laughing,
so hard I think he'll empty out,
but no, the laugh goes on.
It just gets fainter down the street.
Once the last remembered house blinks out
it's all dead reckoning,
whimsy or currents, wind, a lazy minutehand
as I think my way past any hope of sleep.
This afternoon—what was I screaming right into your eyes?
Poor Richard's Diner down the street
will be dark until morning, ages away,
though in my mind I am already groping
for landmarks:

Oh red and blue town of Statler Cement,
Kozel Iron & Metal, oh Dairy Mart,
oh corner of Crosstown Parkway and Mill
with your two orange newspaper machines,
the Detroit Free Press and the Kalamazoo Gazette—
my mind is newsprint letters cut out of a page of night.
Will things we said leave holes in our morning and afternoon?

2. THE WORST FIGHT IN OUR HISTORY

After a squall, on the beach from Ludington
to Sleeping Bear Point,
the breakers push and drag ashore
the timbers to a hundred ancient wrecks.
Floating stairways. A stove-in pilot house.

When the part of us that feels most alive
rises through the fathoms of the argument,
we look around, we ask how far
our voices carry us.

Did the neighbors hear?
Your face empties out like a room for rent.

February 4: auspicious day for marriage
and repair of ships.

What can we do for each other? Out the window,
across the oceanic lawn
I see a neighbor turning busily away
from the mouth of our quiet
to *his* lawn and *his* flowerbed and *his* house and *his* quiet—

★

—after the age of schooners, after the age of steamers
after the walking-beam engine and the paddlewheel
with good power on the downstroke

but not much on the up,
in the sickening lunges of smoke and pause,
how can anyone have much of an appetite?

But everyone seems to be ravenous.
In the morning a diner is mostly men and smoke,
men who blow out smoke in stale blossomings,

blue anchors, stale hearts drifting apart—
men whose stares dribble nowhere.
How many ages ago did I see a face as if through wavy glass?

What day was it, what time, whose face?

I want to make a date with your sleeping face.
Tomorrow morning. You and me
our greasy eggs and American fries.
We'll tell our dreams
though probably not quite *to* each other's eyes.
Let each one sail his lack of narrative
as if there were a port
in all that fog.
Or will I have slept enough to dream?
Sleepless nights blink red in the window,
morning is an empty parking lot.

I want to ask your face across the fish-tank of a booth:
whose name is advertised on the coffee cups
floating toward us on a tray?
Is it yours or mine?
Which one of us is Kozel, Statler, Crosstown, Mill?
Poor Richard will be wiping the counter
the way he always does,
between the booths there will be those troughs
where it gets all quiet
after the gale-wind blows
for the early shift. Across the silences
of dollar bills tucked under plates
I will remember this
dream about owls up in the trees.
They are screeching
here I am.

3. A History of Navigation

Sometimes in a squall
the pouring of storm oil on the water
doesn't work. Then the wind goes whistling
over the forty- and fifty-foot crests
and the gloomy cook goes sloshing around in the ship's galley
stacking pots and pans on the highest shelf.
Each time
we turn the volume up, then down, behind the words,
we weep, we make of sweet relief our peace,
we scan the windows for superlatives: *One of the most daring*
pieces of expert seamanship
in the history of navigation!
To voyage over water, to make our way—
let's lie in bed in the hour of shipwrecked laughs,
one awake and one asleep,
and steer past the first or last
jalopy backfiring in the alley.

Poor car, poor town,
roar down inside us and sleep.

from *Poetry Northwest*

A Night Without Stars

◇　◇　◇

And the lake was a dark spot
                 on a lung.
Some part of its peace was dead; the rest was temporary. Sleeping ducks
       and geese,
goose shit underfoot
                and wet gray blades of grass.
The fingerlings like sleeping bullets
                              hung deep in the troughs of the hatchery
and cold traveled each one end to end,
such cold,
       such distances.

We lay down in the grass on our backs—
beyond the hatchery the streetlights were mired in fog and so
there were no stars,
              or stars would say there was no earth.

Just a single homesick firefly lit on a grass blade.
Just our fingers
          curled and clutching grass,
this dark our outmost hide, and under it
                     true skin.

from *Alaska Quarterly Review*

Sleeping on the Bus

◇ ◇ ◇

How we drift in the twilight of bus stations,
how we shrink in overcoats as we sit,
how we wait for the loudspeaker
to tell us when the bus is leaving,
how we bang on soda machines
for lost silver, how bewildered we are
at the vision of our own faces
in white-lit bathroom mirrors.

How we forget the bus stations of Alabama,
Birmingham to Montgomery,
how the Freedom Riders were abandoned
to the beckoning mob, how afterwards
their faces were tender and lopsided as spoiled fruit,
fingers searching the mouth for lost teeth,
and how the riders, descendants
of Africa and Europe both, kept riding
even as the mob with pleading hands wept fiercely
for the ancient laws of segregation.

How we forget Biloxi, Mississippi, a decade before,
where no witnesses spoke to cameras,
how a brown man in Army uniform
was pulled from the bus by police
when he sneered at the custom of the back seat,
how the magistrate proclaimed a week in jail
and went back to bed with a shot of whiskey,
how the brownskinned soldier could not sleep
as he listened for the prowling of his jailers,

the muttering and cardplaying of the hangmen
they might become.
His name is not in the index;
he did not tell his family for years.
How he told me, and still I forget.

How we doze upright on buses,
how the night overtakes us
in the babble of headphones,
how the singing and clapping
of another generation
fade like distant radio
as we ride, forehead
heavy on the window,
how we sleep, how we sleep.

from *The Progressive*

Rednecks

◇ ◇ ◇

Gaithersburg, Maryland

At Scot Gas, Darnestown Road,
the high school boys
pumping gas
would snicker at the rednecks.
Every Saturday night there was Earl,
puckering his liquor-smashed face
to announce that he was driving
across the bridge, a bridge spanning
only the whiskey river
that bubbled in his stomach.
Earl's car, one side crumpled like his nose,
would circle closely around the pumps,
turn signal winking relentlessly.

Another pickup truck morning,
and rednecks. Loitering
in our red uniforms, we watched
as a pickup rumbled through.
We expected: "Fill it with no-lead, boy,
and gimme a cash ticket."
We expected the farmer with sideburns
and a pompadour.
We, with new diplomas framed
at home, never expected the woman.
Her face was a purple rubber mask
melting off her head, scars rippling down

where the fire seared her freak face,
leaving her a carnival where high school boys
paid a quarter to look, and look away.

No one took the pump. The farmer saw us standing
in our red uniforms, a regiment of illiterate conscripts.
Still watching us, he leaned across the seat of the truck
and kissed her. He kissed her
all over her happy ruined face, kissed her
as I pumped the gas and scraped the windshield
and measured the oil, he kept kissing her.

from *Ploughshares*

BETH ANN FENNELLY

Poem Not to Be Read
at Your Wedding

◇ ◇ ◇

You ask me for a poem about love
in lieu of a wedding present, trying to save me
money. For three nights I've lain under
glow-in-the-dark stars I've stuck to the ceiling
over my bed. I've listened to the songs
of the galaxy. Well Carmen, I would rather
give you your third set of steak knives
than tell you what I know. Let me find you
some other store-bought present. Don't
make me warn you of stars, how they see us
from that distance as miniature and breakable,
from the bride who tops the wedding cake
to the Mary on Pinto dashboards
holding her ripe red heart in her hands.

from *Farmer's Market*

In This Place

◇　◇　◇

Within
the dark bowels
of this prison, the walls rise
twenty feet, blocking out the sun.
Creating a cement and steel tomb for the living,
whose life of hell is never done. No quiet or solitude,
yet always alone, trying to keep sanity in place—a hard
task for any person who has to wear a mask to cover
all emotion. Within the dark bowels of this prison,
the animal instinct needed to survive exists
in each prisoner's heart and mind,
as he continues his lone fight
to stay alive.

from *Extracts from Pelican Bay*

Salmo: Para El

◇ ◇ ◇

for Marisela Norte

Yo soy Joaquín
el que nunca ha ido a México
el que no habla ni inglés ni español
el Pocho
el Macho
el que se identifica como revolucionario
el que tiene como profession
ser subersivo
el poeta patriarchal
el que habla por la madre tierra
el que cuenta la historia
de la gloria Azteca

I am Hispanic
He is herpanic
He is the Latin Boom
the Mambo King
Ricki Ricardo
Black Narcissus
Black Orpheus
el vato Valentino
your Jungle book
your magic realism
your Latin Lover

your cha-cha boy
your gansta boy
your boy toy

He is el Louie
el homeboy
the Aztec Angel
the lowrider of love
the boy that's not the boy next door
el chulo
el que no sirve pa' nada
el vago
el sinvergüenza
el puto
hijo de su pinche madre

El es el hijo
el que va o na va repetir
la vida de su padre
el possible principe azul
el que llama cada noche a la novia
el que sabe referirse a los padres de la novia
con "señor y señora cómo están ustedes esta noche?"

Yo soy el niño bueno
el que siempre va a misa con su madre
el que toma comunión y quiere ser padre
el altar boy
el pobrecito
el prietito
el feito

El es el chico moderno
medio Almodovariano
pues se cree muy postmoderno
el es experto en el uso de condones
el que está en moda
el que sale a bailar cuatro veces por semana
el que no tiene que responder a la cuestión—
"¿Y tú, quién eres?"

pues todo mundo lo sabe;
que él es la Moda
lo más reciente

El es el hijo bueno
el esposo
el que es buen trabajador
al que le gusta la cerveza Coors
el padre
el que no va a misa
al que le gusta mirar deportes
en la televisión
el que nunca habla con sus hijos
el dueño
el jefe
el viejo
el que manda
el que juega cartas
y va a los gallos
el mujeriego
el padre
el Señor
Dios
el Cristo Cósmico

El es el héroe
el mero mero
el santo enmascarado
Blue Demon
el superhéroe
el Che Guevara
el illegal alien
el mojado
el que el no puede ser
Yo
el primitov
la violencia, la belleza
la oscura transgresión
the voiceless
pure silence, empty space

the writing on the wall
the blood on the ground
no soy nadie
soy el responsable

from *The Americas Review*

Two Girls

◇ ◇ ◇

who come in the night whispering
Whose songs are too small to remember
Whose rest Whose gestures disappeared
To look for them without a sentence
To make a shelter for them here
One night dance One firstlight singer
Who mark each lost nearness with tears
One torn cloth coat One pact unmended
Who warn in whispers fifty years
One who wants the word for morning
Two we think are here no longer
One who wants the word for footprint
Two girls tangled in the branches
One in smoke One in shadow
One from bridges One from snow
                              Kaddish
The languages of wrists and ankles
Winter Soup Bread A woman's neck
Sealed train to suddenly an island
Here she who lay down her small flesh
This crow This star This metal bramble
This path where craft and bodies mesh
This night chimney This ditch This shamble
To manufacture smoke from breath
What you know of masks Of making
Forest clearing built of ashes
Nachtwache The word for footprint
All the songs you have forgotten
This ghost fury This disguise

Borrowed mouth and borrowed eyes
at exactly 8:15 a.m. a thousand doves released from cages
Mountain flanks Barley Delta bridges
Salt river's movement in the heat
Summer Daughter Breakfast Two fishes
Shadows The language shadows speak
A cricket Just before the brightness
She who watches She who has seen
Invention heralded by engines
This labor's fruit This planned machine
Straw umbrellas Coats of paper
Temples choked with unclaimed ashes
Thirst *Zensho* The word for morning
She who could not keep her skin on
You who call her No Witness
You who think she found her rest
                                          You
Her hair smoothed back from fever forehead
Her chill in nearness put away
The fledgling kept The sapling guarded
These two who knock with every rain
Where there is warmth Where there is water
The stamping songs of yesterday
Two guardians Two raging daughters
You who were taught another way
You who think a word is useless
You who mock and doubt your dreaming
You who know dirt is not holy
You who never were a child
Archipelago Cistern
You hungry You thirsty Turn

from *The American Voice*

Nachtwache: nightwatchman
Zensho: conflagration

Kapital

◊   ◊   ◊

Hooking boxes of dogfish
across the packinghouse floor,
take the fat grease pencil you
use to mark 36/BOS or 42/NY
on the split-pine boxlids
and draw a circle around
the place where *labor* becomes
surplus or where my stepfather's
cigarette, thirty cents a pack
in those days, went sparking
from his lip when his boot
hit the wet ice, when he went
under the wheels of the forklift:
Three cents a pound, twenty thousand
pounds, packed in ice and stacked:
Take your allowance for boxes,
the box-makers in their wire cages
pumping pedals, take your
allowance for diesel, take
the boat's share, the owner's
two shares, the skipper's son's
half-share, take making that ripped
pair of gloves last another week,
take him hot soup and bread,
take him his worthless union card
and his thermos of coffee
and his watchcap over his ears:
You can't save him—he only
wanted to come home to a hot supper,

hash and eggs in the blackened pan
and then lean against the iron stove
to warm his back before bed.
But there's nothing you can do
in your small child's terror
when the woman says, *What
will we eat? How will we live?*
You *will* eat and you *will* live,
this time, in this life, though
in other times, you have perished,
and on winter mornings thereafter
you have risen to the lunch pail
and drifted along the glazed wharves
and reckoned your wage on your fingers,
your hard eye drawing its essential light
skyward from the idle trawlers
while they locked and buckled
in the freezing harbor.

from *The Kenyon Review*

White Beach

◊　◊　◊

for D.Y.

Once in a while in the sounds of wind and voices
there is some story of us, and the sound of making love

when both persons are inside it. I didn't know that, then,
when we all were too young to know because even if

we had done it we have never yet been inside it.
At the Freeport beach each of us was his body, or hers;

it was as though, forced or willing, we were put on display to each
            other
by our species, that was sorting us for reproduction.

Sunburned and tired, we were on our way home
in the dark after my friend's front teeth were gone,

lost for all time in the Gulf when his surfboard
jumped away from him and then right away found him again

as he was flailing under that last wave in the summer-late dusk,
wave he shouldn't have ridden anyway. Even so,

he was driving his own car because no one else
was allowed to, but his bleeding had stopped

and the rest of us were already forgetting
that his whole head was throbbing,

we were thinking about each other's bodies,
things we wanted to see in each other.

We were on the unavoidable straight road
through a shantytown where drivers coming back to the city

want to speed up but have to slow down this night
because of the confusion, because drunk on beer and heartache

some young black men are throwing or threatening to throw
bottles, stones, bricks at us, at every car that passes.

Shouts and taunts. We get through that,
it quiets us, but in other cars some of the other white boys

have had enough beer to want to stop and fight
and their girlfriends hang onto them pleading no and love.

And some of the black boys are held back too
by young women with inescapable thoughts of aftermath.

Hurt, harm, what might, what certainly would, be lost,
when our kind convulsed against each other.

(And those who were hurt were often
heroes for it, loved more than others.)

Mile by mile, much too fast, now, we return
to late-night avenues and three-high overpasses.

Hot and dank and subtropical, our half-raised city
is all pretense at reality, the buildings stand

beside the freeways as if they really are solid,
we speed through the late emptiness

of the summer night concocting our alibis
and explanations, in case. We think

about it again and again—we held our breath,
we were taut with fright when we realized what

was happening and cars ahead of us began to stop
and we had to stop and we didn't know that someone

might not run right up to us and heave a brick in or worse,
and one of us already was hurt (and loved for it).

Didn't we know it wasn't at all the same as the other way around—
when white boys like us went out at night to drive

through city wards and outlying shantytowns,
brandishing baseball bats from the open windows

of their cars, front and back, their hands
in a furious grip, their mouths taunting . . .

Coolly he swerved to follow the off-ramp, drifting wide
just the right amount then he cut the turn at the light hard,

the girl he thought he was going to marry
thrown close against him, holding onto him

as he raced his own pain down the last streets of dark houses
to the first drop-off, who was kissing someone

in the back seat, pressing one hand against a thigh,
the other inside it. And in the sound of the night air

blowing into the car and in the injured scents
of green and pink, of fishwater and beer

and mown weeds and waxleaf ligustrum and sweat
and suntan lotion and lipstick and skin

and damp clothes and seasalt and hot paving tar
there was something like the smell of human love and hate

when people are really inside them.
This much I think we all of us did know.

from *The Southern Review*

All
(Facts, Stories, Chance)

◇　◇　◇

To Ken McClane

1.

I'm at no center, big & slack as I am

in my evil nature, in the whole blue funk,

in this for thee & myself—

but source, the argument goes, *gives* denotation,

even our having fanned out can't keep the nomenclature from
        overtaking us

(at which point/s it finds its own level, suggests the argument)—

the attitude is all locations

being temporary are

themselves "fugitive"—

that is all location is the way out (*north*

in the archetype)—

in the long view that that stays in

held back behind the face keeps *it* whole whatever happens—

the rivers flow outward (as it were) getting wide, an incalculable sum

to the spate of water (metaphoric depth & rush),

all locations are emphatic & come

to know one place
& the various landscape here

the variation of the edges here—

        the railroad sits up there on its bridges up through town, one

line crossing others (metaphoric height & rumble),

the headlight on the Niagara Rainbow might find us if we stood just right,

before the tracks curved off toward the frontier at the Falls itself—

I dreamed I saw us on the coast

wading in the Atlantic off Senegal, off Gambia,

the coast of beautiful Gabon or Cameroon, I couldn't tell,

but there were white people on the cliffs above us

the pale voices clearly phrased in the wind

at our backs as usual & waking I saw it had been the dunes on Lake
        Ontario I saw,

that we'd been at the end of Rte 414, at the end of upstate N.Y., that it was Canada across the water,

more ambivalent than we'd thought for an archetype

all invisible etc to be so big

2

In another we walked through a small shopping center near here, the
        far edge

of which was dominated in the dream by a K-Mart store, & out

through the store's dark back-rooms past
                the stacked boxes & the time clock, all
the service doors looked out
on the employees' parking lot & the dumpsters
                but one, which opened

onto a path through tall grass & up

an embankment, across a gravel road
                & then down through the trees under a hillside—

        all the trouble

& misinformation about which door
was which had made us short w/one another & so our faces closed up

getting all exact,

all unhidden & still the shapelessness of, even as we walked on,

the relation to *here,* our source between us at face level

★

(In another the archetypal convict had escaped & it fell to thee & me,
        old buddy,

———
81

to bring him in, we in our Ivy League suits, he

at large—
        When the captain sd "Where's the trail?" we sd "It swam on"

      —yet *we* were ambivalent, of many minds vis-a-vis serving

the state: culture was more than indefinite, it was an archipelago

of colonies, all names

had fled from memory & from the map both,

I saw typescript loose in the air all around our location when we spoke
      in the dream,

the sentences disembodied but readable—

                        (You'd wanted to go start in Cuba
by talking to Guillén about vodun & santéria,

I'd wanted to head back to Dayton, Dayton being curiously the furthest
      back

I was willing to extend, the view being the all-but-truly-Negro country
      SW
of the city proper,

the long view at the apparently stable edge,

the convergence of landscape

along the long roads in

from out of the landscape

—the view past the corporation markers framed by them, the markers—

the ambivalence starting just out there (in memory)

★

                             I'm at no center myself, we were at
in fact, in a *true* story, the edge of Ithaca, N.Y., where

the country comes *in* on hillsides & in triangles

and there 3 black boys were,

feeding a horse grass from the outside of the fence around him—

"Look," I sd as we went by in your Omni on our way

to East Hill Plaza, my long view connected &
detached both,

unrepeating but caught in looking & looking & looking,

in a tendency towards the sentimental,

in a fit

(in a funk),

in the way in & further in at the look itself

of some home or some one

of the metaphorics,

the past's whole long self giving the name

to some thing at loggerheads w/ nothing—

               I'd have disclosed it willingly if I could've

A long song flows out of the future, noise

from no locations, sounding like nothing,

the chance voices edged out,

which were central to it,

not in theory but which waded

through the music as though the singers were looking *for* something

as though the singers were intent on missing nothing

of what they could see in the music

of what they could say in the music:

this was no "universal"—

lost in no old blue woods along the flood at morning,

lost along no railroad under some moon, looking somewhere off
        ahead:

this was not natcheral or unnatcheral either one.

I'm large, though, at

all edges

& pleased at the company on the trip to near home

on the way to near home

which is an unemphatic landscape so

smooth to the eye, a repeating un-

deceptive surface bisected, fanning out,

more than the little intrigue memory is

the agreement sustained
& waiting both, someplace

(everyplace source was

(now music's at the lips,

at soul's opaque & unbroken surface that looked

so smooth from far off,

unimaginably intricate at the thick lip.

from *River Styx*

Possession: A Zuihitsu

◊   ◊   ◊

that mother sat beside my sister, Kei, and spoke to her before any of us knew about her death, told her to take care of father, *go, take care of him,* who was in critical condition but also did not know about this death that only the detectives and paramedics knew, strangers who would transfer news not new to them

that when Kei dances her face becomes the face of her teacher from childhood, so to view her is to no longer see my sister but someone else who moments earlier was the child from my childhood

that as a toddler she would situate herself in the backyard and *knew* where to dig to excavate porcelain doll parts, a glass medicine bottle, a rusted bracelet with the initial D in a private archeology

that my father painted Adam and Eve with Adam's face turned away as his own father turned away from him

that I write without thinking

★

Mine.
No mine.

★

you get your fuckinhands off him girl or you wont have hands for shit

★

"In the end the [warehouse club] industry's acknowledged low-cost operator uses its size and market clout to bleed rivals dry." *Wall Street Journal,* 11/18/93

★

"Retail consultant Peter Monash estimates that Sam's Club cannibalizes itself in 45% of its markets in quest of a dominant market share." WSJ, 11/18/93

★

"[The] idea of using so much cash to suppress [voter] turnout, rather than to increase it, struck many as something new, and odd." WSJ, 11/18/93

★

that when he tests a pen he always and unconsciously writes, *but mom*

that when the five-year-old tantrums she alters her demand as the parent yields: *chocolate milk, too white, not this cup, not this spoon*

★

cleave to the soul

★

when something else is in control of the body—gesture, organs, voice

★

There is a vast difference between private and personal property—one which the bourgeoisie has blurred to antagonize and terrorize the working class. At issue: who owns the means of production, including one's labor.

★

His son died over ten years ago and only now has he resumed consciously writing about the death as surely as grief transforms into *something else. A rocking chair.*

★

turpentine, a sesame bath oil, turkey *soup*—

★

The critic wants her to write identifiably revolutionary (quote unquote) poetry so he can critique it in comparison to his sectarian past rather than explore future possibilities. As we all paddle forward sonically.

★

"The strangest thing was that her robes were permeated with the scent of the poppy seeds burned at exorcisms. She changed clothes repeatedly and even washed her hair, but the odor persisted." *The Tale of Genji* (Murasaki Shikibu, trans. Edward G. Seidensticker), p. 169

★

the dispossessed

★

I saw a red bucket then I saw a red car then I saw a fire hydrant then I saw bricks then I saw a stop sign—and the elephant I lost was red and we'll never find it

★

psychosomatic blindness

★

Whether he traveled or stayed home he could not stop thinking about his deceased wife.

from *Another Chicago Magazine*

Plainsong

◊   ◊   ◊

If your words have become pewter
plain and white, the voice of a Quaker
or a nun, it is because you were a witness
who knew she would not be believed.
Taking a hermeneutic oath
memorizing everything in exact detail,
aware of what all good liars know,
you anticipated every fork
in their arguments like a lawyer
who has stayed up all night with several pots of coffee
and a sheaf of yellow pads.

By the time the birds began,
you would have to have all the facts—
each closing in tight on the next—
because every night at the long shining table
they would say how prone to exaggeration you were
as if they anticipated your courage to speak,
Knowing what you did, you took care to strip
your words of everything pagan and ornate—
no girl's words, no Greek, no looping Southern grace—
paring each one down to its red original skin,
the simple unadorned thing, the only adjective or image
a primary one like an old black and white photograph
with a deckled yellow edge, each member of the family
caught, their white skin ghosting off into the thick
emulsion of the summer air, each word growing
the polish and perfection of ice with close inspection

and what was left was hewed out clean,
so plain as to be incontestable, a kind of witness voice
military in its caution about the power of words.

from *Poetry Flash*

The Prisoner of Camau

◊ ◊ ◊

1.

It was the rustle of nurses that brought him back,
touch of their hands that astonished.
Their voices lulled.

Officers explained his right to counsel.
He told them he starved five years in a bamboo cage
no longer than his body.

Sky fell each night through bars,
bruising like fruit.
A hungry moon pecked the seeds.

Guards dragged him to a hut to sign their papers.
A radio screeched
like an orchestra of crickets.

They cut three fingers off each hand,
leaving two to hold a pen,
two to hold their paper.

He told officers he'd written
an epic of the moon,
plotted an escape through constellations.

An officer asked about weapon dumps,
tunnels beneath the camp,
secrets he may have told.

2.

When he flew to Charleston,
the moon wore a phosphor crown.
Sun smoldered all day on molten streets.

Black smoke plumed from buildings on the news.
His fingers twitched like ghosts
from snuffed wicks.

The local papers got his story wrong.
For months
he lived in another time.

Mortars flared
in ducts above his bed.
Geysers of mud spouted from the marsh.

He woke on a cratered dike.
Shapes flapped like crows,
shouting "Mau di! Mau di! Mau di!"

They bandaged his eyes with a rag,
buried him beneath a tarp
in a sweltering boat.

A pole knocked like a broken clock.
When it stopped, a goose
squeaked in a hamlet near Camau.

3.

In the bamboo cage
fungus etched a map
of jungles on his thighs.

Guards bowed and smiled,
pushing cups of rice
and fried minnows through the bars.

He told himself a story
is a poultice
for shrapnel beneath skin,

retraced the cold canal,
the night march to the paddy,
pigs rummaging beneath the sentry.

Bullets scooped divots
as they ran from rice shoots
toward the smoking huts.

It ended with peonies of flame
on thatch, the platoon
stalking footprints

through banana groves and pineapple fields,
tossing compasses into air
when the mortars hit.

4.

After they wired his hands to a board
hammered the machete through knuckles,
flinging stubs to pigs,

he lay on bamboo poles,
watching ants carry torches
of rice into soft brown bunkers.

A tree shrew entertained
by gathering fish spines into a nest,
until a guard shot it off a mangrove branch.

The moon was delirious,
scratching its skull
to a gray knuckle.

He signed the guard's story
so they would unhook
spotlights by his head.

He plotted stars into a Scheherazade,
composed episodes of radiance and dust,
strolled through the Zodiac.

On old roads in heaven
God gave him ideas
and maps for his journey.

5.

Unwrapping his hand,
he saw his father's ghost,
his palm's crossed life-lines.

A week before his father died
they watched a juggler
on the Ed Sullivan Show spinning plates.

One wobbled
like a gyroscope
and the others crashed.

His father said: "Think of it;
the man disgracing himself
because he couldn't keep his plates up!"

As if planets
had fallen from circuits,
God stumbled from cloud.

He didn't question.
He had been trained
to keep the plates up.

Staring at gray stubs,
he saw his father's hands
on a stage of broken plates.

6.

When the monsoon hit
the jungle flickered,
an old, grainy film.

He lay on a slatted mat
wondering how to hang
from a noose braided from straw.

Would the bamboo break?
Would a guard cut him down,
pare off thumbs?

He decided to build
a *hacienda del sol*
night by night.

He spent days
planning every room,
every picture and plant.

In principle
it was a sun dial.
Shadows climbed the walls.

Every morning he built new walls
between the cage's bars
from gathered stars.

7.

To celebrate its completion
he scratched a baseball diamond
on the bottom of a tin cup,

marked first base,
second, third, and home,
poked a hole for a bamboo splinter.

Spinning the dial
to determine hits,
keeping score with rice grains,

he played two full seasons
before guards decided he prayed
to a battered chalice.

He invited them to his batting cage
filled with stars:
Mantle, Williams, Cobb, Ruth.

They took front row seats
for the World Series,
razzed him through bars.

During the final game
he faced each batter
until all the stars struck out.

8.

Practicing his knuckle ball,
he saw a helicopter
scattering guards into elephant grass,

signaled to the pilot
who swooped toward the baseline
outside his *hacienda del sol*.

He wanted to forget
like the river
sloughing its brown skin in trees,

forget the candle stubs
of hands,
his name on the guards' story.

At the hospital he drew a blueprint
of his *hacienda del sol*,
its rooms reserved for stars,

confessed ants and a tree shrew
had saved him,
and his epic of the moon.

that his father's ghost
had spoken
of fallen plates.

9.

In Charleston
pushing a cart
through a frigid Piggly Wiggly,

he heard a boy:
"That man has lobster claws!"
He dropped a milk jug into lettuce.

In the parking lot
wandered in a haze of sweat
unable to find his car.

That night he woke in a bamboo cage.
Fingertips crawled
like slugs through fishbones.

He reached for them
scribbling dust
beneath the tree shrew's whimper.

At dawn he rowed from the Battery,
ghosts of planters
rocking on porches.

He held up his hands,
stared at pink and gold mansions
rising from the stubs.

from *Beloit Poetry Journal*

The Steadying

◊　◊　◊

Where we are, & at what speed: I know
we're spinning 14 miles a minute around the axis
of the earth; 1080 miles a minute in orbit
around our sun; 700 miles a second
straight out toward the constellation Virgo;
& now Custer is charging maybe a half-
mile a minute into an Indian village; but
from many eyewitnesses we know
Crazy Horse dismounted to fire his gun.
He steadied himself, & did not waste ammo.

Where we are, & at what speed: I saw
on display at Ford's Theater in Washington, D.C.,
the black boots & top hat Lincoln wore that night;
at Auschwitz, a pile of thousands of eyeglasses also
behind glass to slow their disintegration;
in a Toronto museum, ancient mummies, ditto;
in Waikiki, some glittering duds once worn by Elvis; but
from many eyewitnesses we know
Crazy Horse dismounted to fire his gun.
He steadied himself, & did not waste ammo.

Where we are, & at what speed: I remember,
in Montana, a tumbleweed striking the back of my knees;
when I was a boy, a flock of blackbirds & starlings
beating past Nesconset for the whole morning;
at Westminster Abbey, in the stone corner, a poet's rose
for just a second drinking a streak of snow;
cattlecars of redwoods vowelling to Gotham in my dream; but

from many eyewitnesses we know
Crazy Horse dismounted to fire his gun.
He steadied himself, & did not waste ammo.

from *TriQuarterly*

Renewal

◇   ◇   ◇

This empty Monarch stove and rotting birch aren't much excuse
for my stack of stinking beer bottles. But we do have the snow,

the cars on snowpacked pavement, exhaust in subsequent taillight,
and I want to crack open my fingers, hear nothing

of argument or image, as pure song spills out and fills the room.
Maybe February enters this town with the clarity

of a child's hands, and the lighthouse stands to its knees
in black waves, searching the last cloudbellies before the horizon,

scanning as if some lover might be sailing Superior home tonight,
after all these years. This much alone'd be a sight.

Still, a fine desolation refuses to mix our casualties
with the first blood of the Ironwood girl as she runs

from a barn into a field, twisted junk cars abandoned
like her father's lovers, in a wreckage of the corn.

And if we belong to the Midwest only as abstract
expressionists, it's all the same. We live here

with lake effect piling in our yards. The snow moves through us
without lights and blasts between suspension wires at night

above the Mackinac Bridge, sticking in hundred-foot-tall strands.
And the band covers Pure Prairie League every Thursday, nine to close.

Out at the empty county airport where all the flights are cancelled
blue points strobe in time up the landing strip just in case.

Up in this gable room, the greatest possible bravery
is a hairbrush of yellow spider-web at dawn.

We always toy with hopefulness, splatters
of yellow dot my dark wood floor like dandelions

above all the empty setting, the people living there
under a ceiling of expected snow. Without me,

they sleep. But a few old ones eye the night like crushed food
they still can chew. And shove it in their mouths.

from *Cream City Review*

Reading Aloud
to My Father

◊   ◊   ◊

I chose the book haphazard
from the shelf, but with Nabokov's first
sentence I knew it wasn't the thing
to read to a dying man:
The cradle rocks above an abyss, it began,
and common sense tells us that our existence
is but a brief crack of light
between two eternities of darkness.

The words disturbed both of us immediately,
and I stopped. With music it was the same—
Chopin's piano concerto—he asked me
to turn it off. He ceased eating, and drank
little, while the tumors briskly appropriated
what was left of him.

But to return to the cradle rocking. I think
Nabokov had it wrong. This is the abyss.
That's why babies howl at birth,
and why the dying so often reach
for something only they can apprehend.

At the end they don't want their hands
to be under the covers, and if you should put
your hand on theirs in a tentative gesture

of solidarity, they'll pull the hand free;
and you must honor that desire,
and let them pull it free.

from *Poetry*

Two Canadian Landscapes

◊ ◊ ◊

1

And so Diana visited a tavern called *Diana*
on a night the wind hurt most.
Her three curs pawed and sniffed the filthy snow;
their red lop-ears looked sore in the neon glow.

Shoulder to heel and the span of her filled the door.
Her hurdler's thighs were taut.
Among mortal women only the char is allowed in,
then, after hours, not with a bow but a mop.

Yet here stood the virgin, adored by a treacherous god.
The pool game ceased.
Above her breasts three small tattoos:
      a stag   a date-palm   and a bee.

No beer was forthcoming.
Out of her quiver she drew an arrow
with a shaft of silver, feathered crimson and gold.
She sent it the bar's full length.

A quart of lager burst at the neck.
Outside her hounds snapped smoke.
The great cross shone from the highest hill in town.
Above that, the moon.

II

Warm night fog and the smell of pulp
on the wind
          as mill lights in the distance
flicker, fitfully as stars.
Close on March
after the season of rains, front
upon front drubbing cove, spit and seawall:
even crows scarce,
forsaking their perches
when the tumbling sea shook a great fir log
from its sandy notch.
                The mind flutters,
aloft on contrary winds
that pull together skies and then tear them apart.
            Crocuses
in thick husks inch up.
Clusters of them advance as the shank of winter
retreats inland.
        The rain
begins falling again, softly,
an occasional foghorn,
cats' nimble couplings on wet grass:
                         spy
in a strange city—
spring.

from *Private*

Nude Study

◇   ◇   ◇

Someone lightly brushed the penis
    alive. Belief is almost
        flesh. Wings beat,

dust trying to breathe, as if the figure
    might rise from the oils
        & flee the dead

artist's studio. For years
    this piece of work was there
        like a golden struggle

shadowing Thomas McKeller, a black
    elevator operator at the Boston
        Copley Plaza Hotel, a friend

of John Singer Sargent—hidden
    among sketches & drawings, a model
        for Apollo & a bas-relief

of Arion. So much taken
    for granted & denied, only
        grace & mutability

can complete this face belonging
    to Greek bodies castrated
        with a veil of dust.

from *The Kenyon Review*

STANLEY KUNITZ

Touch Me

◇ ◇ ◇

Summer is late, my heart.
Words plucked out of the air
some forty years ago
when I was wild with love
and torn almost in two
scatter like leaves this night
of whistling wind and rain.
It is my heart that's late,
it is my song that's flown.
Outdoors all afternoon
under a gunmetal sky
staking my garden down,
I kneeled to the crickets trilling
underfoot as if about
to burst from their crusty shells;
and like a child again
marvelled to hear so clear
and brave a music pour
from such a small machine.
What makes the engine go?
Desire, desire, desire.
The longing for the dance
stirs in the buried life.
One season only,
                    and it's done.
So let the battered old willow
thrash against the windowpanes
and the house timbers creak.

Darling, do you remember
the man you married? Touch me,
remind me who I am.

from *The New Yorker*

N A T A S H A   L E   B E L

Boxing the Female

◇   ◇   ◇

I saw myself inside again I saw
myself inside a box
which had no bottom, front
nor face only
sides, four, closing
in at right angles and me
crouching low
within the dark
interior
I saw myself inside again I saw
myself a box inside
which kept me as I
grew and grew
too large and round for this or
did the box continue
to shrink and tighten
into a passionate
claustrophobia
I saw inside again myself I saw
a box inside myself
I was open
and unclothed without
hair or
shadow to hide my
feminine geometry
which molds and holds
the woman I was then that I am
now
but it was so so dark where it was bare

where I was
uncovered lying undiscovered there
fragile and awkward in the iron emptiness
I began and I
begin
coming out of myself again I am
coming into my form
my born body new and
gravid with musical sensuality
strong and proud
from deep inside this box I am
no longer kept I am no longer
held as precious token beauty
nor quiet prize nor secret pleasure I am
my own ugliness
outside this dark hard fist
of walls and corners crushing
my living mind, the blooming
human pattern of my chemistry
through pouring rocks of ferocious
silence
that you impose I will
turn over
my bones inside my skin and
shatter
these walls with my song I will sing
my ripe real me out loud
with body and heart and brain
all beating against each other
in a heightening passion and I am
opening
this box for you for
myself I am the naked light inside.

from *Hanging Loose*

NATASHA LE BEL

Foot Fire Burn Dance

◇   ◇   ◇

I do the black boot stomp
on my stucco ceiling
late at night
sometimes
when I think of songs
I write in my head
they beat beat beat up
inside my head breaking
out my eyes and ears
All my winter fever rises
and shoots out through
my pores
to peel the air around me
back and let this new heat expand and
rush
I do the black boot bang
on my thin thin walls
when no one is listening
to crack the paint and
let the music sealed inside
come pouring out
so I can swallow it whole
and in my fury
take it down to my feet and
give it life
I do the black boot thud
on my blue carpet floor
when the fire engines passing by
don't pass

and I hear the sirens
anyhow
I find fire in my feet
beating and burning and
thudding and churning music
out my soles
in my black boot stomp
hard breaking
the angry night

from *Hanging Loose*

Kolohe *or Communication*

◇ ◇ ◇

1. While he strategies in rush-hour traffic I mention to my husband
   that the night before, I asked my eighty-five-year-old mother if
   she and father enjoyed "good sex."

> Directly, he commands
> (without shifting his focus from driving)
> "I don't want to know."

"Good"
(I set him up).
"I don't want to tell you anyway."

2. Complaining while washing dishes mother hints that
   "Your father asked my father for my hand in marriage
   in Hawaiian."

> —What did these two *guys* say to each other?
> Was it the Chinese or Hawaiian phonemes that lyricized each other's
> greed and passion to inherit instant *aliʻi huangdi?*
>
> (Take a breath!)

> Was it a moment of Smithsonian-level *haku mele?*

Ai ya! Ai ya   *Auwē*   *pilikia*   auh huh.
(You know *kaona*. You know what they were doing.
You know they were up to no good.)
Did they graft Chinese concept into Hawaiian
erotica?

> Was it the *mana? aloha?* Or, a matter of
> lust for   lust?

How about the issue of *kālā, chyan:*
the MONEY.
Did they drink? Mustve.

Did daddy promise not to be Hawaiian to gain his
bride?
Did grandpa see a sanction to wiggle his hopes and
serenade his beautiful young wife at any possible
occasion?

     Pretty pretty
grandma. Petal skin   beauty mark lilting above the curve of her left lip
nearly bald
from every day pulling the hair into the black flower.
Knock your wind out, body goes
limp when you see the photo of her.
Something inside her body   pulls your nose up to her picture
stirs your logic.
"So so pretty   even after twelve kids."   *My* grandma.
Mona Lisa mouth
butterfly eyes.   Bones.
No stereotype doctor or teacher. Poor. A slave all her life. No agenda.
That smile: Look, you can tell.
                   My 99.9999% Han man
                   only dreams that he had grandpa's luck.

Sweet young grandma who despised grandpa when
he did the hula and flirted in Hawaiian.

Nice grandma who loved me most because
                  (everyone in the family will nod and know)
I was the worst. I *needed* the most love.
I was unpure; white and Hawaiian
I pulled her bun
Tied her in knots to her hospital bed and wound
the bed into a V while cheating at Chinese checkers.
I stole her silver dollars and big-ass fifty-cent pieces.
I tickled her
When she screamed and threatened, I tickled her more.

We rocked and rolled in the cuckoo's nest
feeling like grandpa when occasionally, he turned Hawaiian.

3. Announcing to my Chinese husband one morning
   I am Hawaiian

> That pagan. Third-World immigrant. That low-level cadre's kid
> grabs me by the shoulders and shouts his law:
> Carolyn Lau is Chi-nese!

> "Not now. No," says Carolyn Lau
> Not any more.
> I'm sick of Chinese.
> Don't bother *trying* to have a good time around Chinese:
> you have to wrestle the eternal frown inside their imaginations.

> Insulted, I repeat "I am Hawaiian."
> Days later, post-sex snacks
> my hero regrets no longer being the svelte prince he scaled
> when he first charmed me.
> Undaunted, I support his feelings by encouraging him that
> > I rather like his fatty and *share*
> > when we make love,
> > I pretend he is Hawaiian.

> This knight is uncertain if he should strangle or
> cherish me for *our* sense of humor.

> On another occasion, commenting how he could not sleep one night,
> I assure my husband that
> > in the very spot where he tossed and turned,
> > my Portuguese boyfriend had earlier snored.

4. When I went home to Hawai'i, flowers perfumed the house   aunties
       joking and
   wisecracking day and night   *pīkai* light rain   Vietnamese Chinese
       Japanese
   Portuguese Korean Hawaiian Filipino Puerto Rican—all kinds of food
       smells
   sexualizing the balmy heat of salty air and sweat

My husband is now home in China enduring a reality check and bit of cognitive dissonance.
Cheap tight shoes bargain brown bananas (I warned him. So what?)

5. Footnote:

Nervous Chinese: who make me scared, and then sick.
Hawaiians cued to channel 88: constant vibrators.

Chinese glean idea from crown of skull.
From the stomach: Hawaiian.

China is Oklahoma in the late 1920s.
Hawai'i breaks your back but the weather is an item.

When did the blues thrill my loss with China?
When I married a Chinese who ate peppers and sang like James Brown.

New Fairbank, new Kanahele: the dialectic presses on.

The translation:

In church, my father and I pray Catholic.
Chinese grandma snickering loudly pagan.
With my sister and Hawaiian grandma, I pulse 'aumakua

To be my body, I solve my head into two cylinders
stretching the sky to my stomach. There, white columns finish a toilet
that flushes energy somewhere else.

When I can't become the owl or shark the vessel that breeds this flesh;
locates forms and single out sound as words for aloha—

in between the battles of language—

the mango tree and ginger and pikake
mo'olelo   mana'o

like Ovid's Metamorphoses, Kumulipo blesses man's misadventures.

Through words, breath and heart exceeding definition,

Kolohe—the answer laughter

kolohe
for what?

Kolohe, for no particular reason.

GLOSSARY

kolohe   mischievous
ali'i   people of high social rank
huangdi   emperor
haku mele   to compose a song or chant
auwē   alas
pilikia   trouble
kaona   double meaning
mana   power
aloha   a feeling of being opened to all elements
kālā   money
'aumākua   family or personal guardian spirit, often taking the form of an animal
mo'ōlelo   myths
mana'o   desire, thought, or wish
Kumulipo   the Hawaiian creation chant

from *Manoa*

It Is Not

◊ ◊ ◊

We have the body of a woman, an arch over the ground,
but there is no danger. Her hair falls, spine bowed,
but no one is with her. The desert, yes, with its
cacti, bursage, sidewinders. She is not in danger.
If we notice, there are the tracks of animals
moving east, toward the sunrise, and the light
is about to touch a woman's body without possession.
Here, there are no girls' bones in the earth, marked
with violence. A cholla blooms, just two feet away.
It blooms.

There is a man, like her father, who wakes to a note
saying *I have gone for a day, to the desert.* Now,
he believes she is in danger. He will try to anticipate
what happens to a young woman, how it will happen, how
he will deal with the terrible. In him, he feels
he knows this, somehow, he knows because there are men
he knows who are capable. This place she has gone, where?
But it doesn't matter. There is, first of all, the heat
which scorches, snakes with their coils and open mouths,
men who go there with the very thing in mind. The very
thing.

It is the desert on its own. Miles. Beyond what anyone
can see. Not peaceful nor vengeful. It does not bow down.
It is not danger. I cannot speak of it without easing
or troubling myself. It is not panorama nor theater.
I do not know. It is only conception: then fruits
like gifts or burdens I bear. Whether arch, a prayer,

or danger. They can happen, yes, we conceive them.
This very woman I know, the man does sit tortured.
The desert, created, embodies its place, and watch us
lay our visions, oh god, upon it.

from *Prairie Schooner*

The River
and Under the River

◊　◊　◊

At dusk every day, our cattle leave the river,
single-file, trundling their weight to the upper pastures.
And, every night, the river is left to itself, infertile
and self-loathing, most beautiful when it comes close
to absence; its grooves and grottoes hum
with the noise of a landscape's slow consumption.
If I put my ear to the ground
could I hear the drag of the river turning
limestone into silt? Would it tell of Carlos pulled
through water on a slim and muscley night at Turnhole Bend?
I want to know the missing part of his story
that ends with the flush of foxfire on a grave—
as if from the body's heat fading out
Tonight the river is at work dissolving, solving
over and over the riddle of its loosening. I want to know
how to hear it, and what it might teach me:
how to inhabit this thing of bone, gut, and blood,
this part of me that would not vanish if I vanished.

from *No Roses Review*

Edge Effect

◊   ◊   ◊

Aracdia Beach, Oregon

The zone where two communities overlap, called an ecotone, shares char-
acteristics of both communities and therefore is diverse. That is, the edge of
a community is more diversified than its center, a phenomenon also known
as "edge effect.". . . The region where the land and sea overlap . . . is one of
the best examples of edge effect in the world.

Allan A. Schoenherr,
A Natural History of California

Even under a petroglyphic coastal overcast,
the sand flushes with a heat almost innocent,
unhurt as it burns, and thus it is so often
the purest place for us as children.

Now, when we imprint its edge, we know it will wash.
While we may squint, *its* glint is broken lenses.
Rubbing sand in my palm, I feel
vision in that hand. I see

to reach outside the wet breathing ribcage
of the horizon. At my blind side,
basalt: shearable, towerable, and able to abide
long hours and average eons. The cliff

houses its resident eyes in caves,
in nests, down crevices, in hives. Ships,
if sensitive, may feel watched. And underfoot,
beneath goat-stepping wet opals of old toenails,

whole orbits of washed-in sea gooseberries
kindle a gaze up every few feet, glassies
convexing the vista, oculists' models of the eye's
hermaphroditic twin, paired in one single flesh

as we, with two eyes in one head, are mated for sight.
Merely to move forward, I tear draglines
of gull prints, their scuff's slight stickiness
to land before they fly. Beneath gulls' high ride,

every second villager's the best imagist
he or she can be for sea stacks' rough allure
offshore. It's all the brush-fingered seem to see.
Their garden or kitchen studios hatch water-slender

watercolors, stout sumi-e outlines, stolen styles—
expropriated eyes—of great but landlocked artists
of any continent but this. They line the palisades,
hold mirrors to the sea, even gladly to fog.

The whole subduction zone
calls painters for a briefing every day—
and every day the wet description dries.
But here, far up the littoral, I feel another congregation;

I sense they are inspecting everything going by.
Backbone, backbone, backbone
of stones: Stack three, you have a god; a minor one
improves on none. It's a beach outing

for a gang of almighties. Each has a base, a trunk, a head,
a jutting chin. Or driftwood eyebrows.
They are more than pillars, rock on rock.
One probes with seaweed field glasses, alert with poise

not of the spy but of the curious, of the
minerally secure: What's to be seen, its body
language says, in this shred of humanity coursing
north? I feel weather-cut edges of one watcher

multiply, its brain stones' ordained postures aiming
at the sea through any shore-searcher in the way.
I feel stone necks risen to attention, each vertebra
an observation deck. Against the cliff a pantheon.

No shadows on their cheeks, they are not grim.
Gray, they are not whimsy. They stand up stark.

What does "stark" mean anyway? Didn't Anne G. say
my father-in-law George's weightroom

"looked so stark?" Those dumbbells no longer made,
their deadweight laid out in increments
of hardship, increasing as hardship will, the barbells
propped like desolate businessmen at the final gate

of an airport concourse, present only to pick up
another drear and cunning company joe
whose name they hold penned on a pitiful placard. . . .
Stark. Can it mean pure? utter? simple? strong?

Sometimes I've seen eighty-year-old George standing
on his head, upside-down power, a restacking
of stones, right there on his gunboat-stern
cement basement floor, rebuilding, rearranging the cairn,

his body well-trained to be ancient, an Old World
stonemason. Why should bone be the most
solid-seeming part of a god around a mind?
Isn't a skull just a showcase for eyes? The fact that feet

in air come down, rocks tumble in time,
deduce to abdomen, thorax, small insect head,
almost back to diagram, that one
frost crystal brings the stone church to the ground,

excuses or defends erecting this toppler
while one can. Gods *are* hard. But longer life-tested sand
is soft. I hear one rock fall, the highest stone, on point,
fall backwards, and here we turn, we must turn, back,

as we would if we had any children with us,
not ready to take them beyond the falling of the gods
and yet permitting them to hear
the softness of their landings,

where wounds will bathe, bedded in sand,
one edge rushing over to enfold the other.

from *Poetry*

JAMES MERRILL

b o d y

◇   ◇   ◇

Look closely at the letters. Can you see,
entering (stage right), then floating full,
then heading off—so soon—how like a little kohl-rimmed moon
o plots her course from *b* to *d*

—as *y,* unanswered, knocks at the stage door?
Looked at too long, words fail,
phase out. Ask, now that *body* shines
no longer, by what light you learn these lines
and what the *b* and *d* stood for.

—from *The New York Times*

Lament for the Makers

◇   ◇   ◇

I that all through my early days
I remember well was always
    the youngest of the company
    save for one sister after me

from the time when I was able
to walk under the dinner table
    and be punished for that promptly
    because its leaves could fall on me

father and mother overhead
who they talked with and what they said
    were mostly clouds that knew already
    directions far too old for me

at school I skipped a grade so that
whatever I did after that
    each year everyone would be
    older and hold it up to me

at college many of my friends
were returning veterans
    equipped with an authority
    I admired and they treated me

as the kid some years below them
so I married half to show them
    and listened with new vanity
    when I heard it said of me

how young I was and what a shock
I was the youngest on the block
    I thought I had it coming to me
    and I believe it mattered to me

and seemed my own and there to stay
for a while then came the day
    I was in another country
    other older friends around me

my youth by then taken for granted
and found that it had been supplanted
    the notes in some anthology
    listed persons born after me

how long had that been going on
how could I be not quite so young
    and not notice and nobody
    even bother to inform me

though my fond hopes were taking longer
than I had hoped when I was younger
    a phrase that came more frequently
    to suggest itself to me

but the secret was still there
safe in the unprotected air
    that breath that in its own words only
    sang when I was a child to me

and caught me helpless to convey it
with nothing but the words to say it
    though it was those words completely
    and they rang it was clear to me

with a changeless overtone
I have listened for since then
    hearing that note endlessly
    vary every time beyond me

trying to find where it comes from
and to what words it may come
  and forever after be
  present for the thought kept at me

that my mother and every day
of our lives would slip away
  like the summer and suddenly
  all would have been taken from me

but that presence I had known
sometimes in words would not be gone
  and if it spoke even once for me
  it would stay there and be me

however few might choose those words
for listening to afterwards
  there I would be awake to see
  a world that looked unchanged to me

I suppose that was what I thought
young as I was then and that note
  sang from the words of somebody
  in my twenties I looked around me

to all the poets who were then
living and whose lines had been
  sustenance and company
  and a light for years to me

I found the portraits of their faces
first in the rows of oval spaces
  in Oscar Williams' *Treasury*
  so they were settled long before me

and they would always be the same
in that distance of their fame
  affixed in immorality
  during their lifetimes while around me

all was woods seen from a train
no sooner glimpsed than gone again
    but those immortals constantly
    in some measure reassured me

then first there was Dylan Thomas
from the White Horse taken from us
    to the brick wall I woke to see
    for years across the street from me

then word of the death of Stevens
brought a new knowledge of silence
    the nothing not there finally
    the sparrow saying *Be thou me*

how long his long auroras had
played on the darkness overhead
    since I looked up from my Shelley
    and Arrowsmith first showed him to me

and not long from his death until
Edwin Muir had fallen still
    that fine bell of the latter day
    not well heard yet it seems to me

Sylvia Plath then took her own
direction into the unknown
    from her last stars and poetry
    in the house a few blocks from me

Williams a little afterwards
was carried off by the black rapids
    that flowed through Paterson as he
    said and their rushing sound is in me

that was the time that gathered Frost
into the dark where he was lost
    to us but from too far to see
    his voice keeps coming back to me

then the sudden news that Ted
Roethke had been found floating dead
    in someone's pool at night but he
    still rises from his lines for me

and on the rimless wheel in turn
Eliot spun and Jarrell was borne
    off by a car who had loved to see
    the racetrack then there came to me

one day the knocking at the garden
door and the news that Berryman
    from the bridge had leapt who twenty
    years before had quoted to me

the passage where *a jest* wrote Crane
falls from the speechless caravan
    with a wave to bones and Henry
    and to all that he had told me

I dreamed that Auden sat up in bed
but I could not catch what he said
    by that time he was already
    dead someone next morning told me

and Marianne Moore entered the ark
Pound would say no more from the dark
    who once had helped to set me free
    I thought of the prose around me

and David Jones would rest until
the turn of time under the hill
    but from the sleep of Arthur he
    wakes an echo that follows me

Lowell thought the shadow skyline
coming toward him was Manhattan
    but it blacked out in the taxi
    once he read his *Notebook* to me

at the number he had uttered
to the driver a last word
        then that watchful and most lonely
        wanderer whose words went with me

everywhere Elizabeth
Bishop lay alone in death
        they were leaving the party early
        our elders it came home to me

but the needle moved among us
taking always by surprise
        flicking by too fast to see
        to touch a friend born after me

and James Wright by his darkened river
heard the night heron pass over
        took his candle down the frosty
        road and disappeared before me

Howard Moss had felt the gnawing
at his name and found that nothing
        made it better he was funny
        even so about it to me

Graves in his nineties lost the score
forgot that he had died before
        found his way back innocently
        who once had been a guide to me

Nemerov sadder than his verse
said a new year could not be worse
        then the black flukes of agony
        went down leaving the words with me

Stafford watched his hand catch the light
seeing that it was time to write
        a memento of their story
        signed and is a plain before me

now Jimmy Merrill's voice is heard
like an aria afterward
	and we know he will never be
	old after all who spoke to me

on the cold street that last evening
of his heart that leapt at finding
	some yet unknown poetry
	then waved through the window to me

in that city we were born in
one by one they have all gone
	out of the time and language we
	had in common which have brought me

to this season after them
the best words did not keep them from
	leaving themselves finally
	as this day is going from me

and the clear note they were hearing
never promised anything
	but the true sound of brevity
	that will go on after me

from *Poetry*

JANE MILLER

Far Away

◇ ◇ ◇

there is weeping, as is

customary and good, the lively sitting on boxes

inside the boxed complex overlooking the bridge.

I shall have to sacrifice one of my few intakes of air

to drag him into the coffin room

and choose the right oak. Come ye,

hear the weeping in and of New Jersey,

the chosen bent earthward ransacking the woods,

unprepared for the tide and wind

until I am like unto him,

American, Jewish, prosperous, and free,

except for death, the freeway below

blasting and blowing us senseless

over a meal. Mud-tongued I pray

his soul be blessed and returned to work

so that which is decent and innocent

shall not be torn limb from limb from me as I dig

deeper into debt and longing, and, thereafter, despair.

Holy the father and memorable his merciful acts

of the hearth and household, laboring

fruitlessly in the unstocked and, when stocked,

uncategorized warehouse, the Bronx

of our sorest complaint, who shall be judged

according to his deeds on earth and his thoughts

and his dreams and his offspring, o especially

those stock phrases and incantatory lines

we represent on earth as we are in heaven, rotten

little verses transformed by the innocent, the decent,

the good and the young into hymns

of detonated twilights along toxic shores,

decent, innocent songs about nothing, nobody,

who lived nowhere and had no neighbor, no

lover, no children, no poetry.

from *Colorado Review*

Girl Tearing Up Her Face

◇   ◇   ◇

Where it's rubbed out, start there, where it's torn
where something like a burn in cloth the hot
metal pressed too long, forgotten

                                    in paper the worm-
hole, the eaten up, the petal frayed browning
at the edges the flower's
flesh like cigarette paper

consumed by the breath sucked back into
the body: yes, body, that's what
that is what—no, I'm not stalling   body

is what I mean to talk about, what I have
on my mind   in my mind   my mind
in the body   of the body

and what's disturbing, yes, that above all: the joy
right there in her face, the girl's, as if she
had been smacked with it, the big fish joy

a cold hard wet smack by something flailing out, this
joy thing throwing itself around

or as if someone had thrown a pudding, a thick batter
and now her face was trying to work its way
through that mess, yes, joy, the mess

the ugliness of it because it has not yet
been practiced, the mouth trying out
positions before the mirror   the mouth

performing little sounds up and down the scale
of pleasure   the joy not yet prepared
for anyone else to look at   the shock like

a flashbulb going off, a camera
pouncing before one is ready   before
one has run the tongue over   taken a bite

out of the smile   hands arranging the hair
the girl looks all doors open, the sheer
weight of her coming starting

to come and her body sucking it back
inhaling each tooth of bliss
running her fingers up and down the comb

It's that ugly I want to rub my face in, that
blossoming, as if a tree had suddenly—
that stamen pushing up out of

the petals, the throat of the apple, its
woods and the dark seeds
bursting the blossom, so I push

her back, I open her mouth right there
where she sits on the swing
a rage of delight shivering the tree's—

can I say flesh, can I say skin?—and
I can't bear to look at her
doing that, it seems too private, as if she

had been caught having a dream she
didn't know she was having
all her wings run over by pleasure, joy

having a tantrum all over her, this
limp rag of beaten down, and the photographer
thinking, Yeah, this is it, the moment

he wants to last and last—the forever: now with
the girl falling asleep on the swing,
her sleep in full view, its lids

pulled open so the deep anaesthesia
of her pleasure is suddenly visible, sucked
inside out so he can hear every sound

a face can make and it's those sounds
he wants to shudder down on, those
cries with the flesh still

attached to them and what they have
been pulled from gaping and
ragged and this is what will be handed

to the girl in black and white, this face
which in two seconds would have
changed and gone on changing, this face

she never suspected and of course, she'll have to
rip it into pieces and keep ripping
because even now I can't bear

to look at her suddenly awake, I want
her asleep again, unbegun, unstarted, the shades
drawn so I can float every which possible, all

manner of across her face accommodating
as a lap, and I don't think
For God's sake, she's only eleven, what does she

know or understand of anything? I'm—I'm flooding
even as she rips herself in two, even as
she vows never to be this person

I'm putting my head down in her lap, pushing
her back on the swing with so much force—
What could split open? What could eat her up?

from *The Paris Review*

Mangos y limones

◇   ◇   ◇

This is a story about transformations, about swellings
and slick slidings, about bodies that grow
and others that slide out wet, like *mangos,* gold
flesh fermenting in salt water, about a woman biting
into the salty juice alive on her tongue, filling her
mouth, piece after piece until, in her friend's small kitchen,
she finished the entire glass jar, smiling and chewing
in silence, her friend's mouth and eyes open as wells.

This is a story about daughters and what they know
of the dark, about her youngest who felt the unseen,
knew at fifteen what the woman herself did not know,
her body, casual in its bleedings, relying on nausea,
reliable as any pregnancy test, but this time no curdling
when she ate tortillas and white cheese warmed in the sun.
"Ay los hombres," she concludes, "they're different
even before a speck of them is visible."

This is a story about lemons, twenty-five she bought
at the *mercado,* tart yellow moons she dug into salt
in her palm, chewing lemon after lemon on the bus home,
lips hungry and open, unlike that youngest daughter whose lips
shut for months, whose eyes grew smaller and smaller
as the mother's body expanded, the girl who ran into the dark
room at the first cry, pressed the newborn, slick as peeled
fruit, to her breast and said to him, "You were killing me,"
who after chasms of silence brought her mother a cup of hot
chocolate sighing, "Mami, I suffered. *Es mio.*"

The mother thinks of them back in El Salvador,
when she slices *limones* or peels *mangos*. Yellow
scents pucker her memory, awaken her mouth then
and its cravings, the aching for fruit and hunger
for grains of sweet salt. Her body thicker now,
she slides a slice of *mango* between her lips,
laughs about once eating twenty-five frosted lemons,
her mouth full of her own stories.

from *Prairie Schooner*

ALICE NOTLEY

One of the Longest Times

◇ ◇ ◇

My brother's always in the gully
Too ugly for me down there
But in the vacant lot next to the house
I pile towels on a creosote bush in the corner
We all go in and sit
Does it smell like creosote oil and have flowers like stars

Albert Margaret and me, holding sacred things here
Sticks and rocks
Small black-scored rock is
The quantum life-story object, take it
Life's beginning and over compact in your dirty palm

We're huddled in here don't need anyone we're
Star-sent-out light that's still alive
We're still here sending out us
As stars from the first world melt
Why aren't we the same as each other
Rocks look the same I'll never be you

This rock's me from before the flood and after the fire
This rock's you and what happens to you it adds up to
This rock this time and
This time this time and
This time in this bush is long, long
Becky's our baby our sister and this one
Is hers from before the flood

And after the fire that comes
I am a rock in these shadows who
Am I speaking to who am I speaking

I got this me. This one's you. What's the point
It would be better if
We all died together
We put and put rocks; I have life coming (life's
Nothing but THIS minute
Something for you a brown stick for you)

This is the longest one of the longest times
It lasts after we're dead and after all people
Are dead; how do you know
Because thoughts have lasted since the first thought
'Cause I think that we're in the first thoughts still
Lasting and we last
And we last, making real selves

from *Fourteen Hills*

The Small Vases from Hebron

◇　◇　◇

Tip their mouths open to the sky.
The turquoise, amber,
the deep green with fluted handle,
pitcher the size of two thumbs,
tiny lip and graceful waist.

Here we place the smallest flower
which could have lived invisibly
in loose soil beside the road,
sprig of succulent rosemary,
bowing mint.

They grow deeper in the center of the table.

Here we entrust the small life,
thread, fragment, breath.
And it bends. It waits all day.
As the bread cools and the children
open their gray copybooks
to shape the letter that looks like
a chimney rising out of a house.

And what do the headlines say?

Nothing of the smaller petal
perfectly arranged inside the larger petal

or the way tinted glass filters light.
Men and boys, praying when they died,
fall out of their skins.
The whole alphabet of living,
heads and tails of words,
sentences, the way they said,
"Ya' Allah!" when astonished,
or "ya'ani" for "I mean"—
a crushed glass under the feet
still shines.
But the child of Hebron sleeps
with the thud of her brothers falling
and the long sorrow of the color red.

from *Many Mountains Moving*

The Eighth
and the Thirteenth

◇   ◇   ◇

The Eighth of Shostakovich,
Music about the worst
Horror history offers,
They played on public radio
Again last night. In solitude
I sipped my wine, I drank
That somber symphony
To the vile lees. The composer
Draws out the minor thirds, the brass
Tumbles overhead like virgin logs
Felled from their forest, washing downriver,
And the rivermen at song. Like ravens
Who know when meat is in the offing,
Oboes form a ring. An avalanche
Of iron violins. At Leningrad
During the years of siege
Between bombardment, hunger
And three sub-freezing winters,
Three million dead were born
Out of Christ's bloody side. Like icy
Fetuses. For months
One could not bury them, the earth
And they alike were adamant.
You stacked the dead like sticks until May's mud,
When, of course, there was pestilence.
But the music continues. It has no other choice.

Stalin hated the music and forbade it.
Not patriotic, not Russian, not Soviet.
But the music continues. It has no other choice.
Peer in as far as you like, it stays
Exactly as bleak as now. The composer
Opens his notebook. *Tyrants like to present themselves as*
patrons of the arts. That's a well-known fact. But tyrants
understand nothing about art. Why? Because tyranny is a
perversion and a tyrant is a pervert. He is attracted by the
chance to crush people, to mock them, stepping over
corpses . . . And so, having satisfied his perverted desires,
the man becomes a leader, and now the perversions continue
because power has to be defended against madmen like
yourself. For even if there are no such enemies, you have to
invent them, because otherwise you can't flex your muscles
completely, you can't oppress the people completely, making
the blood spurt. And without that, what pleasure is there in
power? Very little. The composer
Looks out the door of his dacha, it's April,
He watches farm children at play,
He forgets nothing. For the thirteenth—
I slip its cassette into my car
Radio—they made Kiev's Jews undress
After a march to the suburb,
Shot the hesitant quickly,
Battered some of the lame,
And screamed at everyone.
Valises were taken, would
Not be needed, packed
So abruptly, tied with such
Frayed rope. Soldiers next
Killed a few more. The living ones,
Penises of the men like string,
Breasts of the women bobbling
As at athletics, were told to run
Through a copse, to where
Wet with saliva
The ravine opened her mouth.
Marksmen shot the remainder
Then, there, by the tens of thousands,

Cleverly, so that bodies toppled
In without lugging. An officer
Strode upon the dead,
Shot what stirred.

How it would feel, such uneasy
Footing, even wearing boots
That caressed one's calves, leather
And lambswool, the soles thick rubber,
Such the music's patient inquiry.
What then is the essence of reality?
Of the good? The mind's fuse sputters,
The heart aborts, it smells like wet ashes,
The hands lift to cover their eyes,
Only the music continues. We'll try,
For the first movement,
A full chorus.
The immediate reverse of Beethoven.
An axe between the shoulder blades
Of Herr Wagner. *People knew about Babi Yar
before Yevtushenko's poem, but they were silent. And when
they read the poem, the silence was broken, Art destroys
silence. I know that many will not agree with me and will
point out other, more noble aims of art. They'll talk about
beauty, grace and other high qualities. But you won't catch
me with that bait. I'm like Sobakevich in* Dead Souls: *you
can sugar-coat a toad, and I still won't put it in my mouth.*

Most of my symphonies are tombstones, said Shostakovich.

All poets are Jews, said Tsvetaeva.

The words *never again*
Clashing against the words
Again and again
—That music.

from *Poetry Flash*

Harlem Suite

◇ ◇ ◇

1.

Silent, the Savoy,
where we once danced.
Dim, the Dawn Casino, where we played—
Minton's, Small's Paradise, the Renaissance,
Count Basie's, and the midnight promenade . . .

Of yesterday, what's left
but still, Red Rooster mornings,
dreams of Sugar Hill and Strivers Row,
the after-glow of Monteray and Connie's Inn,
of Baby Grand and Mandalay and Wishing Well and Wonder Bar,
and cool Alhambra nights
at Shalimar and Silver Rail and Lafayette and Odeon
—O Tree of Hope!—
and magical Apollo?

2.

When my soul is weary—
    Do, Jesus!
When my heart is troubled—
    Yes, My Lord!
When my mind don't know my name—
    Have mercy, if you please!

When my soul is weary—
        Mount Calvary!
When my heart is troubled—
        Oh Salem!
When my mind don't know my name—
        St. Philip, on my knees!

I go to Church—
        Mother Zion!
        Shiloh!
        Abyssinian!
Just as I am—
        Christ of the Apostolic Faith!
And the Church cries,
        A-A-A-A-MEN!

3.

Over my head—
above the siren wail,
above the incense, oils of Zion, grilled
        sausages, glistening like a bright disease,
above the open trucks where dreadlocked
        fruits and vegetables prevail,
above the mother tongues of Wolof, Harlemese, Igbo, Creole,
        Gullah, Rasta Patwa, Urdu, Spanglish, Cochin, Arabic,
        Cantonese,
above the drum of hiphop, gospel, reggae, rumba, highlife,
        blues, and gangsta rap,
above the shout of Malcolm, Marcus, Martin, Adam,
        Winnie, Nina, Sharpton, Farrakhan,
above the Congo River crowds of color
        splashing sidewalked traders, sandaled, beach umbrellaed,
        docked beside their battered vans,
above the corridors of kente, dayglow T-shirts, watches,
        sunshades, footwear, masks and statues, earrings, hats,
        cassettes, carpets, books, posters, polished brass and
        cowrie, herbs and nylon hair,

above the gridlocked avenues of heroes,
     late and hurrying towards African Square,
above the helicopter drone, where whispered
     radar beams interrogate the air

—a cry that will not cease:
No Justice, No Peace!
No Justice, No Peace!

4.

Four centuries of
practiced devastation
brought to its current
perfection.

From that cage of fire
such beauty springs,
as takes the breath away!

from *Drumvoices Revue*

As From a Quiver of Arrows

◊　◊　◊

What do we do with the body, do we
burn it, do we set it in dirt or in
stone, do we wrap it in balm, honey,
oil, and then gauze and tip it onto
and trust it to a raft and to water?

What will happen to the memory of his
body, if one of us doesn't hurry now
and write it down fast? Will it be
salt or late light that it melts like?
Floss, rubber gloves, a chewed cap

to a pen elsewhere—how are we to
regard his effects, do we throw them
or use them away, do we say they are
relics and so treat them like relics?
Does his soiled linen count? If so,

would we be wrong then, to wash it?
There are no instructions whether it
should go to where are those with no
linen, or whether by night we should
memorially wear it ourselves, by day

reflect upon it folded, shelved, empty.
Here, on the floor behind his bed is
a bent photo—why? Were the two of
them lovers? Does it mean, where we
found it, that he forgot it or lost it

or intended a safekeeping? Should we
attempt to make contact? What if this
other man too is dead? Or alive, but
doesn't want to remember, is human?
Is it okay to be human, and fall away

from oblation and memory, if we forget,
and can't sometimes help it and sometimes
it is all that we want? How long, in
dawns or new cocks, does that take?
What if it is rest and nothing else that

we want? is it a findable thing, small?
In what hole is it hidden? Is it, maybe,
a country? Will a guide be required who
will say to us how? Do we fly? Do we
swim? What will I do now, with my hands?

from *The Atlantic Monthly*

Song of Calling Souls

(The Drowned Voices from the *Golden Venture*)

◇   ◇   ◇

So here we are
     in the evening darkness
     of Rose Hill Cemetery
gazing out from our ghosts
     like the homeless outside windows.
No moon,
     the spring not the spring of the old days.
Our bodies not ours,
     but only bodies rotting
     in the grave of *laofan*.
We look at the sky
     the earth
     and the four directions.
The storm gathers in
     from all sides.
How shall we pass through this night?

The wind comes blowing.
     We six
in deep shadow
     stand at the end of time,
stand in the night
     that is not just an absence of light,
but a persistent voice,
     unsteady and formless,
hum of summer crickets.

Something wants to be said,
     even if our words
grasp the air in vain
     and nothing remains.
Our story has set a fact
     beyond fable
Our story
     has no beginning or end.

"Home" we say,
and before we utter we utter the word,
our voices choke with longing:

     The cliff of Fuzhou
          studded with stiff pines.
     The waters of Changle
          shadowed in the sway of bamboo.
     Sea and sky fused.
          Mystic fires along the shore.
     Fishermen's dwellings everywhere

          How lovely!
          How familiar!

When dusk falls,
     faint seagull cries.
Blue smoke rises
     from red-tiled roofs.
Small boats offshore
     and fishhawks in silhouette.
Salty winds
     carrying the murmur of reeds.
Tide roads of the sea.

The scenes grow in memory,
scenes we lived day by day,
paying no mind:

Generation after generation,
    nets cast into the lingering light,
    seeds planted in the morning mist.
Fishing kept us out on the waves.
Farming bound our women to the soil.

But at times
    we heard a voice, a promise,
        a golden dream.
Things seen and heard
    turned to confusion.
We pulled our boats onto shore,
    left our wives and children
    behind the mountain's shadow.

From village to village
    we bought and sold
anything at hand
    socks underwear suits and dresses gold even drugs
seven days a week
    three hundred sixty-five days a year
and not just for the money:
    the yearning for adventure
    ran deep in our veins.
We played hide-and-seek
    with the government and police.
When we got caught and lost all our earnings
    we called ourselves "Norman Bethune."
If Mao were still alive
    he'd have surely praised us
    as he did that Canadian doctor
    who gave his life
    helping us fight the Japanese ghosts.
We were glad
    to help build a "socialist" China
    with our illegal gains.
Anyway we had a good laugh
    over our losses.

Still, waves of desire
          rose daily,
this voice luring
          from the far side of the sea.
Not that we yearned for gold
          or worldly delights,
but this voice
          first muttering
                    then roaring in our heads.

So in hope and fear we fared.
          In tears we fared.
Mist spread a veil
          till ocean-bound.
Pinewood mirrored
          in deep green.
At the bottom of the *Golden Venture*
          we did not see our women weeping
          did not hear our children calling.
Only the cry
          "Kari, kari . . ."
of wild geese.

We sailed the ocean
          in the hold of the *Golden Venture*—
                    pigs chickens dogs snakes,
          whatever it was they called us.
Our bodies not ours
          sold to the "snakeheads" for the trip.

You ask why we did this?
          Ask the geese why they migrate
                    from north to south,
          why the eels swim thousands of miles
                    to spawn in the sea.
Tides of desire
          rise for no reason.
So we fared with the faith

New York had more *fu* than Fuzhou,
people there enjoyed "perpetual happiness"
like the name of *Changle.*

So we sailed with the belief
        we could buy ourselves back for $30,000
            within three years.
        Our hard work would bring freedom
            to the next generation.
        Our sons would be prosperous and happy,
            not like us, cursed
            by our own country, cursed
            by the "old barbarians."
        America needed our labor and skills
            as much as we needed its dream . . .

And here we are,
        hovering around this New Jersey cemetery.
Our bodies gone,
        but our blind souls still hanging
            like curtains soaked in rain.

                Our summer clothes so thin!
                So thin our dreams!

Hovering,
        that dark night near Rockaway,
our ship finally heaving into sight of New York.
In thirst and hunger we waited.
In fear and hope we waited
        to be lifted from the ship's hold
        and alight on the land of paradise
"Jump," we'd been told,
"once your feet touch American soil
        you'll be free."
In the dark rain we waited.
"Jump," someone shouted,
"the ship is sinking, the police are coming!"
So we jumped
        into the night

into the raging sea,
our breasts smothered
by foam and weeds,
our passions tangled,
the breath beaten from our bodies
by despair and hate.

Oh, we've sunk so low!
We've sunk so low!

Only to rise again
for clinging to wrongful things.
Easy to sink
in the fire of desire.
Regret comes after the deed.
Sorrow!
Sorrow stitched into the cloak of our souls.
Our former days now changed,
leaving no trace.
The distant mountain lies alone.
Shadows of the city so far away.
Sorrow!
We can speak only in weeping,
memory nothing but white hair on the heart.
Condemned to wander,
lost among the roots of our six senses,
gazing at New York,
gazing homewards,
Fuzhou's mighty waves roiling through the night,
bride in green unveiled in scarlet chamber,
lovers' pillows joined like Siamese twins.
Who can avoid sorrow in this world?

Our legs lingering
in the dew-drenched grass
here and there, still clinging.
This deep night,
is it outside-this-world?
Our women and children
still awaiting our return.

But here we are,
         nameless,
In life and after life,
         apart.
Our song is the crane
         calling in her cage
when she thinks of her young
         toward nightfall.
Will it reach Fuzhou and Changle
         and stir souls from their sleep?
On the boat
         we were close,
hundreds of us in the hold
         jammed in and in.
Here we live even closer,
         six bodies in one hole,
the earth sifting into
         our common grave,
unmarked,
         no stone erected
then crumbling.
         Sands of the shore
may reach an end,
         but not our grief.

Home, oh go home!
         an empty wave.
Ten thousand voices,
         broadcast the pain.
         Please, oh please
call our names
                    Chen Xinhan   Zhen Shimin
even if you can't
         say them right
                    Lin Guoshui   Chen Dajie
even if you don't know
         our origin or age
                    Wang Xin   Huang Changpin
Please, oh please
         call us.

162

Raise our shadows
    from the moss.
Be gentle
    as you call our names.
Do not wake us by force.
    But call us.
Do not let us fade
    from this place,
unlit and unfulfilled.

from *Sulfur*

Poet

◇   ◇   ◇

for Thebe Neruda

1/MMABATHO

You
come in the myth
night hour. There are pages of
dreams in your mother's eyes.
Your
father reads them
with blood-rinsed
memories: exiles and exiles
ended.

The
obituaries of gun
shots welcome you.

The
plow of a martyr's blood
designs furrows in a rising
sun.

This day
is a stool for
you to climb/a
Kente cloth in
side your brain.

2/JOHANNESBURG SHELL

There
are no crabs in
side/here. No softness
commingled/with leisured
strides. No squinting
eyes. No tentacles of
bone. This is a place of
steel. Here. Spears
crumble/fall like the home
lands.
This
is the New Age. This
is the cross
roads instructed
properly. This
is the day/you named
after. The poet's
tough tale scaling
history. To give
Chile Allende's
peopled vision. Words
are bullets here. Words
are periods here. This is
the end/of a sentence.

3/NEW DAY

Hector Petersen's spirit
will use Modibo's pen
to sign the new constitution.
Soweto's children wrote it
with MK ink. They used
Sachs' blown away
arm as quill. Then Hani's
spirit ignites flames
for the ceremonial
rite. Registering/memory

for The Election. Tambo's
soul votes Amandla!
From where Kotane, Nokwe,
Ruth First, Biko and
LaGuma, live in dreams.
A nation carries inside
its heart/beats.

You
come in the myth
night hour. The day
you/touch. Owns part of
dead roots of passion in
side your land. That revives
in your laughter, Thebe. As
the poet in your veins
ascends a mountain. To
trap the condor of your being.
As you soar.

You
were born with blues.
With an ANC imprint
on them. How you gon
do anything but rule?

I will
counsel your parent.

You
come in the myth
night hour.

When the Spirit Spray-Paints the Sky

◊ ◊ ◊

for Moagi, 1994

I/saw you
break
rivets/of the split
personality/of fear.

The
work
ethic/of
the spirit. Some
where/in your eye.

Blue
collar/lust
for/owner
ship. Sailing
in your veins.

Wanderer.

Blues.

The auction
block/of new
beginnings. You

Bidded paths a
head. Where/you collect
severance pay/from
bondage.

You,
old wanderer.

Got
lyrics/of
history. In cuffs/of
your memory. Heritage
is/an opening
in/your laughter. Where
half/your wives
reside. Forlorn/moons
greet you/with D-natural
mornings/on crutches.
Where/night has a broken
arm/swearing.

I/declare.
Silence weaves/your yester
days/in
to a tortured/load.
Covering
your head.

I/be dog
gone/if your dance
ain't a gathering/place
Where/you spray
paint/the sky.

Say.

I/sell
blues/to its walking
shoes.

Say.

I/peddle
things/the spirit can
not/lose.

Say.

I/got a Monday
half/price
Tuesday/ten cents
off. Wednesday/for
credit. Thursday/for a
pint/of blood.

No
need/talk a
bout/Friday.
Unless/you own
a million/blues
words.

Say.
I/disguise.
my tongue's/travels.
Pull/out
a razor/every
time/I cry.

Cut/some
body/when I scream.

I/take
my lyrics/of history.
From memory.

I/was a slave
but/my blues.
Collected rent/from
the master's mind.

My
songs walked
from Mmabatho, Mississippi.
I/hoboed
on/midnight
lightning/at the cross
roads/of Hedacol and Lord
have mercy. I/got off
at/Hallelujah Boulevard.

Dead.

Drunk and
broke. Took/a Jitney
wind/over Pepper's
where/Muddy Waters
listened/to a
long distance/call.
And/I found the thrill
that/was gone.

Reached
in/my eye
sockets. Shot/the other
mule/kicking
in my/stall.

I/dress
in/a brand-new
self.

from *TriQuarterly*

Sestina for Jaime

◇　◇　◇

The woman and the boy look back at the years
They have spent together. At what she will leave: the river,
The Santiam that flows cold
From the mountains over its bed of rock
Into the wide Willamette, warm in the summer;
And the sound roof and sturdy walls of their house.

Now that they have more or less deserted this house—
He only sleeps in it; she plans to return in some years—
Now that she will not plan their summer
Around work whose reward is to lifeguard at the river,
Now that she is walled behind an official sort of rock,
And he has come to find the water uninvitingly cold,

He remembers her holding back, afraid of the cold
Water, reading instead on the boat dock; how the house,
A few hours each day, got painted; and the rock
Cliff with its rope where for years
His friends had swung out over the river
Into the deep pools of summer.

She remembers him in the freedom of summer,
And his friends, teeth chattering from the cold
Plunge into the green flow of the June river,
When he alone could coax her from the house
Where she hid out, from what, for years,
He did not know. Their life was like the rock

Walls of the Santiam Canyon, he thought: Rock,
River, Mother, Son, sun, swimming, living for the summer.
She thought they had all the years
Of their lives to buy pizza and cold
Drinks for his friends, pay for painting the house
When they swam too well to need her at the river.

She dreams she has become the flow of the river;
And basking in sun, that she has always been rock;
That she once tried to keep house,
Baking cookies for a human boy. He dreams it is summer;
That he still has a mother holding back from the cold,
And watching, watching him. It has been years

Since he painted the house in summer.
He loads another log into the stove against the cold.
He's added a Zen garden of plants and river rock. It took him years.

from *In Time*

Twenty-One Years

◇ ◇ ◇

That long ago we drove ourselves
To the thermal pool and floated hours
In its uterine calm, naked as newts;
Then hauled our sapped bliss back uphill
To the cheap hotel; and on a bed
That had plainly borne the labors of love
For at least three generations of roamers,
We faced the choice of using the rest
Of our new lulled ease in joining our selves
In a trial knot of mutual skin—
Our excellent hides that were each then fine
As rawhide gets.
                            The trial worked,
Then worked (with frequent repeats and variants—
Newfound knots as brilliant as any
Known to an eagle scout) for the years
Till I was effectively sheared off smooth
Below the waist.
                            Nine years of bearing that
With no loud grumble; and here again
You volunteer what we have left—
Your same hide, seasoned a little but still
As fine as a well-made glove containing
A trusty hand dispensing grace.
     I take it, new as a playground boy
Confronted with the actual dream
Of proffered skin, and offer it
What I have now, the parts that work.
They prove sufficient; you bloom on schedule,

Old faithful mate.
                    Weeks later, basking,
I feel stripped clean still; in service again,
A scow called back from years in mothballs—
Eager to tow, dredge, breast high seas
If that brief duty bears you on
As it does me.

from *The Southern Review*

Domingo Limón

◇ ◇ ◇

In high school I had a friend
Like you had a friend,
The kind since first grade,

The kind you could count on
Not one way or the other,
Just always to be there,

One more name in the morning,
Somebody we would have missed
The way we would have been missed

If we had not come.
Domingo Limón. Sunday Lemon.
You don't forget a name like that.

Mingo rode his face tractor-like
Down the furrow of years
Our growing up took.

He kept his face to the ground,
He kept his eyes to the ground.
He might have grown taller

If he had looked up.
If he had looked up.
That's all.

After high school he grew the goatee.
We saw what it meant
Even if we couldn't say.

In that strap of hair
There was a cruel understanding
If one looked hard enough:

The goatee was a simple rudder.
That's what high school gave him.
A way to move.

That was high school on his chin.
That line was all of us.
It was a small map,

A gathering of meridians, braided,
Descriptive of how to stand straight
In the sand and the water, and among the rocks.

He could not have spoken
His reasons for growing the goatee,
The same way we could not understand.

But it spoke for itself,
This hair he put first toward the world
There on a putting-out of his chin.

When he smiled with his teeth
It was the beginning of the voyage each time,
His teeth like ivory thumbs

Hitch-hiking themselves toward some adventure,
His teeth the many tusks
Worn off a single elephant

Who would not be stopped,
Who came back to the two holes of the gun,
The two holes of his own nostrils,

Because how else does a rudder lead but straight,
And what a good song of a rudder
That hair below his lip was,

That black thing
That kept him going
But would not let him stop.

It was a rudder and a song both
And together they made a motor.
Added to his body it let him be a boat,

His white and yellow and brown teeth
Now a mouthful of women at the prow,
These teeth-women facing each other

In the angular, comfortable way they did,
Dancing a *sandunga* of loose conversation,
The hardy rhythm of blue risk.

Those women who were his smile
They let him move away from the shore.
This smile and the goatee that started him

They sailed him fully from the shoreline,
That goatee becoming a leg
That pushed him from the dock.

It pushed him far and it took him farther
But no one knows where.
It was not on our map.

We don't know the death
Toward which a rudder like that eases a boy
Who just looked like a man,

A boy who was after all the elephant,
Not just the ivory.
He was the elephant

And the boat to get us to the elephants,
And the rudder too.
The boy who was everything

Just small.   Nothing loud.
He was the hero
And the story itself as well

The way in third grade he said he was
Though we laughed because we didn't understand
When he talked to himself.

But he was the hero and the story and us.
And all we could do was watch.
He had no words to tell us what we saw.

He knew we could not know.
It was a plough, finally,
That goatee, that blade into the earth.

He knew we could not hold against our lips
The edge of the plow
Steel on the hip-bone

Tearing up everything,
The whole body under it.
I still see it, Mingo.

from *Prairie Schooner*

Abundance
and Satisfaction

◊   ◊   ◊

1.

One butterfly is not enough. We need
many thousands of them, if only
for the effusion of the wayward-
swaying words they occasion—blue
and copper hairstreaks, sulphur
and cabbage whites, brimstones,
peacock fritillaries, tortoiseshell
emperors, skippers, meadow browns.
We need a multitude of butterflies
right on the tongue simply to be able
to speak with a varied six-pinned
poise and particularity.

But thousands of butterflies
are surfeit. We need just one
flitter to apprehend correctly
the will of aspen leaves, the lassitude
of lupine petals, the sleep
of a sleeping eyelid. To examine
adequately one set of finely leaded,
stained wings of violet translucence,
one single sucking proboscis (sap-
and-sugar-licking thread), to study
thoroughly just one powder scale, one

gold speck from one dusted butterfly
forewing would require at least
a millennium of attention to all melody,
phrase, gravity and horizon.

2.

And just the same, one moon is more
than sufficient, ample complexity
and bewilderment—single waning crescent,
waxing crescent, lone gibbous, one perfect,
solitary sickle and pearl, one map
of mountains and lava plains, Mare
Nectaris, Crater Tycho. And how could
anyone really hold more than one full
moon in one heart?

Yet one moon is not enough. We need
millions of moons, glossy porcelain
globes glowing as if from the inside out,
weaving among each other in the sky
like lanterns bobbing on a black river
sea-bound. Then we could study
moons and the traversings of moons
and the multiple meanings of the phases
of moons, and the eclipsing of moons
by one another. We need a new language
of moons containing all the syllables
of interacting rocks of light
so that we might fully understand,
at last, the phrase "one heart
in many moons."

3.

And of gods, we need just one, one
for the grief of twenty snow geese
frozen by their feet in ice and dead
above winter water. Yet we need twenty-
times-twenty gods for all the recurring
memories of twenty snow geese frozen
by their feet in sharp lake-water ice.

But a single god suffices
for the union of joys in one school
of invisible green-brown minnows
flocking over green-brown stones
in a clear spring, but three gods
are required to wind and unwind
the braided urging of spring—root,
blossom and spore. And we need
the one brother of gods for a fragged
plain, blizzard-split, battered
by tumbleweeds and wire fences,
and the one sister to mind
the million sparks and explosions
of gods on fire in a pine forest.

I want one god to be both scatter
and pillar, one to explain simultaneously
mercy and derision, yet a legion of gods
for the spools of confusion and design,
but one god alone to hold me by the waist,
to rumble and quake in my ear, to dance me
round and round, one couple with forty
gods in the heavenly background
with forty violins with one
immortal baton keeping time.

from *The Iowa Review*

Prometheus
at Coney Island

◊   ◊   ◊

Up over the swell of hot sugar
up over the swell of rubber
Up over the death creaks, rises and falls
like heart attacks
Up over the backyards and bricks
Up over the smell of Ms. Roha's beans
Up over fat men in boxer shorts
Up over the people in ticket stands
Who hate you.
Up over the haunted houses and
1942 ectoplasm.
Up over the Coney Island gray beach,
over the Coney Island gray water that will
make your shins itch.
Up and turning,
circling back over the city, back over pipes
and billboards, pressures and nausea;
our car turns and sways and equilibriums
like greased jets and leather.
Over the swell of hot sugar at Coney Island
they pulled him hard,
under a yellow snow-line:
Gesticulating without talking,
creaking like the shingles of an ancient house,
raising and lowering like breath
sighing farewell to its ancient patriarch

blowing kisses as he's taken away,
like a famed entertainer heaving in the public eye.
                    In the impaling sun
they threw him into the sea of
Pomatum grease,
                    to singe his beard and
rid him of his dirt.
                    Watermelons and pumpkins
were brought, and a pipe of brass to keep cool
his face—so as to show sick
newborn smartness,
                    an avatar
of polka dancers.
                    And laid out was an accordion
and Pannish mouth harp
under which clasped women could dance in the
sand—
moaning over containers overrun with fruit and fish.
Under the figure eights of gulls—
decorating the sand's own dead hills,
lighting fire in the company of thrills,
as was life in the old country.

                    from *Hanging Loose*

For the Evening Land

◇   ◇   ◇

"What causes a death rattle?"
—The New York Times

If there is a sound before death in America
What causes that sound
Asks the newspaper
For most there is no sound
Only a dream of two words: White black
Irreversible or the dream without words
There is no voice in America
Only the finite
Reading the voices
But let me die singing, like the forefathers
Lightning never hits the obtrusive pole,
But the animals shrivel in the field.
And the obscure observer takes a note.
And what is that sound before death—
They have banished the death rattle, the rhonchi, the rales.
We die elsewhere, of something else.
And what is that last sound my mother made
Softly made: archaic breathing. And do not call it a dream.
Nor is it a game: The child says infinity is a small word
We have done away with noise and have left only
The agonal respiration like war material.
You will paint the Americans but is it
The father in a grain of dust, heroic androgyne with honeysuckle
Man in a skirt, woman in a flower, faithless but free
The child thinks the god's birthday must be every day:
He is that old. Fool's gold folly. Crystals slouch out of matrix.

While the spider illuminates his influence with a film
Of joy, the fly develops his refuge in a shattered theme
The dead sunflower almost blocks the sun   .
Like an old poet, an empty eye coerces us
Like an old fate, the gods are dipped in water and predict
Man is red dust, let there be flesh.
There is no sound before death in America
You do not see the charred soldier, only pleasure.
We have done away with all noise, but the agony of respiration.
And autumn will be the flag of that new nation.

from *Lingo*

Crepuscule

◇   ◇   ◇

Yellows cast their spells: the evening primrose
shudders unclosed, sells itself to the sphinx
moth's length of tongue. Again a lackluster
husband doesn't show. A little missus

eases the burnt suffering of a cat-
fish supper, undresses, slowly lowers
into a lukewarm tub. In her honeymoon
nightgown she rolls her own from the blue

can of Bugler, her lust a lamp the wick
of which is dipped in sloe gin. Hands
wander to her hangdog breasts, jaded Friday night
underpants, hackneyed nylon in heat.

Now his black taxidermy outstares her, the stern
heads of squirrel and deer. Now the house confesses,
discloses her like a rumor, vague and misquoted.
From the porch, from the glider she spies rose-

pink twilight flyers—sphinx moths drinking
the calyx, the corolla, the stamen
dry. The stuttering wings, the spread petals
suggest an interlingual breathing, a beating

back of all false tongues. She thinks of the chaw
lodged in his lip when he talks or her husband's
middle finger in the snuffbox and rubbed
along his gum. She walks, wanting him, into the latter-

math, into the primrose, the parched field itching
with critters. She walks, wanting and unwanting
him while birds miss curfew into the thick of the thigh-
high grass, craven and dangerous, in the heavy red.

from *Poetry*

Skin Trade

◇　◇　◇

And then I said, That's what it means
to testify: to sit in the locked dark muttering
when you should be dead to the world. The muse
just shrugged and shaded his blue eyes. So naturally
I followed him down to his father's house
by the river, a converted factory in the old
industrial park: somewhere to sit
on threadbare cushions eating my words
and his promises, safe as milk
that dries the throat. If I had a home,
he'd be that unmade bed. He's my America
twisted in dirty sheets, my inspiration
for a sleepless night. No getting around that
white skin.
　　　　　　He throws things out the window
he should keep; he collects things
he should feed to the river. He takes me
down. While there, I pick them up.

The river always does this to me:
gulls squawking and the smell of paper mills
upstream, air crowded with effluents
like riding the bus underwater. I'm spending nights
in the polluted current, teaching sunken bodies how
to swim. My feet always stay wet. Sometimes
I leave footprints the shape of blood; sometimes glass
flows through broken veins, and I glitter.

Every other step refers to white men
and their names. *Back of the bus with you,*
nigger. They're turning warehouses
into condos, I'm selling everything
at clearance prices: here's a bronze star
for suffering quietly like a good
boy.
      River of salt, will I see my love again?
Cold viscous water holds its course even after
it's gone. Throw a face into it and you'll never look
again, throw a voice and you'll hear sobbing
all the way down. Narcissus, that's my flower
forced in January, black-eyed bells echoing
sluggish eddies. Who hit him first?

The muse has covered his face
with his hands. It's just a reflex
of the historical storm that sired him:
something to say, "The sun is beating down
too hard on my pith helmet, the oil slick
on the river's not my fault, when are you going
home?" What he doesn't want to see, he doesn't
see. In the sludge that drowns the river, rats
pick fights with the debris. He calls them all
by their first names, he's looking through his fingers
like a fence. They make good neighbors. His friends
make do with what they can. They drink beer
from sewer-colored bottles in the dry stream
bed, powdered milk of human kindness and evaporated
silt. They stay by the river till past
sunrise, crooning a lullaby
to help it to sleep. The words
of their drinking songs are scrawled on the ceiling,
Mene, mene, tekel, upharsin: a madrigal
for the millennium's end.
                  I'm counting
down the days in someone else's
unmade bed, let these things break

their hold on me. The world
would like to see me dead, another gone
black man. I'm still awake.

from *Ploughshares*

ENID SHOMER

Passive Resistance

◇ ◇ ◇

Nevada Desert Experience, 1993★

I'm teaching those who will step across the line to be arrested
that language can be violent, too, as yesterday, when they taunted the guide
on the government bus tour of the Nevada Nuclear Test
Site, blamed her for the puddled aluminum homes, the re-bar peeled

off the bank vaults like melted licorice sticks, the craters that look like
　　　the earth
sucked in its cheeks and held its breath. I've given them a "box of words"—
"neon," "casino," "angel"—to keep their righteousness from bursting forth.
I'm reading them my own bad lines to help them over the hurdle

of fear. But I came to Las Vegas with a secret motive—to drop a C-note
for my father, one year dead. I didn't attend the unveiling of his stone,
not wishing to show him respect, knowing that under his coat
of clay, he was still a threat, that his half-life decayed into mine.

Last night I clung to roulette as if to the helm of some ghost ship.
It took three hours to lose sixty bucks. I bet his birthday a dozen
times, won once and pulled ahead. The slot machines rolled ripe
cherries into my lap. My father adored, in the sense of worshipped,
　　　this cousin

★Nevada Desert Experience is an organization dedicated to the witnessing and non-violent protesting of nuclear weapons testing. Several times a year they sponsor workshops and visit the Nevada Nuclear Test Site near Las Vegas.

to Disney World, with its waitresses dressed as slave girls, clockless rooms,
automatic change machines, Glitter Gulch's neon canyons.
Racing form, fishing dock or poker chips, he was always chumming
for luck. That is the gambler's lot—to live in the seconds *before* the dice run

aground on the felt or the racehorse pins the jockey's silks to the wind.
Now my students write faster under the plain-faced clock, cramming all
their passion into eight lines, using ten of the words which do not include
"justice," "bomb," "Nagasaki" or "atomic." Be personal,

I said—complicitous, not haughty. Imagine yourself on the wooden
      bleachers
happy to watch the desert lit from below by the incandescent
palsy of an underground bomb. Invent a science that could prosper
from 800 tests. Is evil a force or a lack, like the shadow that carves
      the crescent

moon? Tomorrow, they'll return to the Site, armed with hats, canteens
sunscreen and towels. They'll alert the police, tape their wrists for the
      handcuffs.
Tonight I'll lose the last forty dollars in a kind of mechanical keening,
playing the slots, craps, roulette again, games without a bluff.

I won't strew a bucket of chips on the floor to watch human
beings grovel, the way that my father would. I'll bet his birthday
      and deathday.
I'll lose without contempt for the gamblers, without resisting the odds,
      doom in
my emptying pockets as I near what must have been ground-zero

for him. I'll offer this peaceful protest against the violence he exacted
as his due. Let these be the last wages of Philip Steine.
Let them be clawed aside by the croupier, squandered like the origami
cranes folded in yesterday's seminar to nosedive onto the hottest
spot in the world while the disobedient cross the line.

from *Poetry*

Fair Trade

◇ ◇ ◇

I did my best when I was young,
Just married, just walking my love
From one room to the next.
I was living in my madness—
The traffic inside
My head and outside
Our downtown apartment, *vatos*
Crucified with blue tattoos . . .
I walked my wife from
One sun-lit room to the next,
And on a dead Sunday
I walked her to the Azteca Cafe,
Slum eating that
Was fried chicken with its rag
Of wings, lumpy gravy,
The anemic coins
Of carrots. My money, then,
Was five dollars tumbled
Through the wash, and coins
Warmed by sunlight
On the chest of drawers.
Money is what gave me
A plate of chicken,
Steam like a glove,
And when I wiped
My glasses, a Mexican man
Was asking for toast.
The waitress turned
And started the order,

Two slices browning
In its stand-up bed
Of red, angry filaments.
When she said, "Sixty cents,"
I thought, two slices
No meat or butter. The man
Hesitated, then fumbled for
Coins from his pocket.
This, I saw, was pride.
I stabbed my carrots,
Hurting for this man.
He took his toast
In a paper napkin,
Toast that was already cool,
And left no trail of crumbs
But the line from my eye
To the bell jingling
On the closing door.

from *Prairie Schooner*

Flight

◇ ◇ ◇

This exists only in my memory
And what I tell you now:
It is cool. The nightwind blows around me.
My fingers wrap the mesh of chain-link fence.
I can smell the metal, smell the grass I'm crushing
And far-off blooming roses, burnt gasoline, rubber.
One by one, the airplanes turn
Then run down the concrete, faster, faster,
Each plane makes a line of light that bends up at the end,
Rising, diminishing into a spark
So small we cannot tell it from the stars.
Once again   I walked in summer fields last night
And watched the lights begin to show in the sky,
Some of them at first identical to the stars
But growing brighter, nearer,
Now clearly seen as planes approaching.
I thought of other nights and other fields
And those who stood beside me watching then
All now dead, everything dead or gone,
The old airfield   long abandoned,
The unknown pilots, crews,
I can shut my eyes and see them, even now.
And the sky, the sky that seems eternal
And so full of fire,
The sky is full of lies.
Stars   burnt out   centuries ago
Whose light still reaches us, and so says science,
But I swear to you
I have felt the electric connections

And I have seen them reaching out, gleaming and strong,
Interlinking, weaving, arching up and out,
Forward and back in time and space
From me to you, from you to me,
Crossing continents and years and seas,
And I have heard and sensed you
And I know you to be there
Tomorrow or today
And how can I refuse
From now until my final breath
Spinning out these signals and these words
Connecting me to you?
I have spent days sunk in despair
Grieving for those I've loved
Walking through empty rooms alone
Feeling presences just beyond sight,
Just beyond hearing,
Hoping and fearing what   a sudden turn around corner
Might reveal (might not reveal).
I have felt each living link begin to wither,
A   feeble signal sometimes coming back,
Sometimes fading away.
Light, sound, energy, matter,
All change but go on.
I have walked the   battlefields,
Old settlements, mounds, medicine wheels,
Trying to find some trace in the ruins,
Trying to catch some signal
That will help me understand,
That will tell me what to do.
Where Etowah Mound rises from the bottomland,
The cornfields tremble with the presence
Of those who came before.
This is a country full of the unseen,
Sounds of birds and flutes
And smell of woodsmoke on the wind
Where no campfire ought to be,
Flowers springing from cracks in the pavement,
Thoughts coming unbidden into unlikely heads:
"Save the whale. Save the planet. Save the snail darter."

Has time a bend in it?
Nothing is lost, they say,
But all shall be transformed.
High above the mists of morning, out of my sight,
I can hear geese calling
As they pass overhead on their way home.

from *Callaloo*

heat

◊   ◊   ◊

hot boys, she says, are sweet in the summertime
muscles burning taut and rippled
steam rising off their shoulders and hanging
in the air, heavy swirling auras of light
and cologne, making a greenhouse in her room
backing away coolly, i say i'm not so sure
with my sour apple gum and dry air-conditioning
(keep me from her heat sticking my hand to my cheek
eternal expression of awe) i watch her try
to bloom, bear fruit, or at least create honey
to boil in the fevered friction, wailing as she rubs up
against them and then they stand, patient shiny statues
sweat gleaming just beneath their skin.

from *Hanging Loose*

ROBERTO TEJADA

"Honeycomb perfection of this form before me . . ."

◇ ◇ ◇

Honeycomb perfection of this form before me.
No, not one imposing megalith, neither harrowing nor laughable
—the Coatlicue stone; or the monumental head of Juárez
by Siqueiros toward the ROUTE-190-TOLLBOOTH to Puebla—
but the infinite combination of matter in myriad flux, each/conduit
a machine in perpetual motion to generate the light
of all cities everywhere:
from this political navel to
the seamless outer fabric and the shadowhands behind
it, every interlocking part on the friezes at Mitla,
a remembered banter, a half-articulated sun
over what I'm getting at,

over these ruined phrases, see,
waking dull with repetition
and then *I vanishes with the dog-lights' sweet breathing*
over the cool wood of summer
and its countless diamonds spilling.

"OK, so I sort of got the environs right as they were rendered
around me. Here now, they just hover in place," in/stead,
a chalk-choke foothold longed for,
rushing down Mexico City's metro, the smell
of burning rubber and baking sweat.

Wait. Not more than twenty miles from here,
in Itzamatitlán, an out-Lawrenced
repulsion—"inexplicable scent, in which
there are resin and perspiration
and sunburned earth and urine
among other things"
—tossed into the dense air
in whose dry-wicker powder
of each page turned verso
from the 5-SUN codex
of what I need to know to make the work-day-week
ennobling, the whole thing
worth it & rage-
wrecked

or watermarked
by yet another PEMEX oil-slick catastrophe
off the coast of Coatzacoalcos when dictation
recedes of a sudden in ebb
& ejaculated glow

from *Sulfur*

Aisle of Dogs

◇　◇　◇

In the first cage
a hunk of raw flesh.
No, it was alive, but skinned.

Or its back was skinned.
The knobs of the spine

poked through the bluish meat.

It was a pit bull, held by the shelter
for evidence until the case
could come to trial,

then they'd put him down. The dog,
not the human whose cruelty

lived on in the brindled body,
unmoving except for the enemy eyes.

Not for adoption, said the sign.

All the other cages held adoptable pets,
the manic yappers, sad matted mongrels,
the dumb slobbering abandoned ones,

the sick, the shaved, the scratching,
the wounded and terrified, the lost,

one to a cage, their water dishes
overturned, their shit tracked around,

on both sides of a long echoey
concrete aisle—clank of chain mesh gates,
the attendant hosing down the gutters

with his headphones on, half-dancing
to the song in his head.

I'd come for kittens. There were none.
So I stood in front of the pit bull's
quivering carcass, its longdrawn death,

its untouched food, its incurable hatred
of my species, until the man with the hose
touched my arm and steered me away,

shaking his head in a way that said
Don't look. Leave him alone.
I don't know why, either.

from *The Iowa Review*

Ghost Sickness

◊   ◊   ◊

this is the sound of poisons
the sickness no one knows
shriekback

I saw the dead nodding sugar skulls.
They danced dark alleys bright
from burning.
Children licked the letters of their names
from glassy candy foreheads. Whorehouse poets
whispered sly reports
to ice cream suited gunmen.

Did you see the federales fall,
spin beneath dry aqueducts and drop,
machine-gunned by four hungry ghosts,
adobe coats punched red in blooded blossoms.

In blackest deserts Pancho Villa headless
sank to hollow knees
to plead with countless sleeping graveyard bones
to take him home, to find the road he could not see,
to fill his empty hands with dreaming.

Antlers of smoke from maquiladoras rising.
Bluecoat children with radium blood
stood at day-long counters hard-
wiring RCA, IBM, ITT, ICBM: 10 cents
an hour: red flowers already in their wombs,
they fought for room at taco stands, the whistle blew

and they flowed, the blue tide of Tijuana,
Tecate, Mexicali, Matamoros. Fat
sputtered and spattered on fuming coals. Old
men drowsed on filth-shined curbs. Sienna cheeks
carved into riverruns of wrinkle: relief
maps of forget.

We followed the Mexican road,
rolled all that dark feathered snake-spine
that looped doomed volcanoes. The sad
sore-backed trucks
hauled tall dust-frosted loads
    lava grit fans
    thrown free
    on loose turns

    would flee
    down the slopes:
        fistfuls of stony whispers.

My dead father at the wheel.
One cool hand on the gears, one gray arm
out the window, cocked: cigarette aimed at the sun,
firing sparks, white whorls
on his smoky muscles
    gone soft in the wind,
        in the grave, loose—
           ripped
               in the wind—
                   he flinched
and the houses
on highway's edge
flashed past,
so many
scattered post-cards—
feverlight
in every door:
grandfathers leaned canes against benches,
women combed rivers from their heads,
parrots flaming in cages.

My father said
There's nothing left.

Children at roadside
shot wooden rifles:
paz-paz-paz: sold armadillos
in small paper boxes: danced
at the brink of barrancas:
lived
13 yards
from the roadside.

We dug as we sped
an unbreachable trench
full of longing,
shadows,
radio music.

2.

I fled this land with The Man.
Northern borders rolled off my barbed-wire back.
My shadow, shredded as a wetback's shirt
still flapping.

How could I become
who I would be: I searched for the future me
in the eyes of men, some signal,
some sign: so mad was I
for manhood.

To be
        a cowboy.
To be
        a big daddy.
To be
        el mero chingon de estos rumbos
        y si no les qusta, les hecho la tierra encima.
To be

        a lover of women.
To be
        a jimihendrix.
To be
        anything but what I was.

What made these men return
each night, dreams dented,
worries tightening as they climbed the steps:
Kiss the wife Set the clock 6 a.m. Pay the gas
Warm the car Shovel snow No sit-ups tonight
Heart attack Cholesterol Pay the rent Lunch box
Cold coffee no sugar little cream
Daughter's puberty Athlete's foot Overtime Fill er up
Dan Rather Graveyard shift Iran Iraq Crack Beer
IRS GMC CBS HUD PMS BVD Bald headed Bad breath
Bad back Bad luck Bad check
and boyhopes
folded under flightless wings.

Did Mexicans trudge home
through bad dream streetlights? My father did.
Until he did
not.

3.

He didn't come back.
He with his manhood smells
I tracked all those miles:
his tobacco smell,
his machinery smell,
his playboy coffee break smell.
His foot powder
his sorrowful
his hungry
angry
lonely

tired
armpit, hair tonic
father's smell.

From the grave to the womb
he fled.

His eyes pure as mirrors
told me
nothing.

4.

Drought killed the cattle. The sun's hard fist
milked them dry, dropped them
in pools of their own shadow.

Waterless.

On highway shoulder, cows
upturned: 4 legs stiff
as furniture. Upholstery gutted
by obsidian vultures: sofas of death
tumbled,
dismantled.

Such heat.

Our lips white paper.
Red calligraphy of laughter.
Such heat
on the land where night
grows thin calluses of snow
on high plateaus gone clear by dawn
to steam.

The road
left a perfect impression of me
cut out every micro-

millimeter of wind,
the moon
rolled thick as an eye
sunburned white.

5.

Down the coast
turtle hunters lay
in seaside shacks
trapped
in wrapping nets
of heat.
Women
bundled in sand
dark breathing
knots of shade.
Dry turtle shells
rocked
in wind,
tocked
like ancient clocks.

The hunters twitched
caught
in dreams
of waves
sunfish
blood.
Hungry men
burned black.
Men who smell sealanes
even in sleep.

for James Atlee Phillips

6.

Alive, he dreamed loud.
He slept in sleeveless undershirts, white pubic hair
a heart-shaped ghost. Two groaning beds, neon windows, fans
chewed flies to slivers, spit
them over us: thin rain
of legs, antennae.

Geckos on the walls
licked spiders from the brick.

And then his dreaming.

He ground his teeth and spun,
a dense pale star
tied in sheets: his teeth
chipped off, they cheeped
trapped in his mouth.
I cringed.
I longed to reach him, slap him
in his sleep, in hotel rooms, at midnight, one
o'clock, two o'clock, three: stretch across that wailing
wall of grief, cry
    stop it, wake up. halt
the grinding shatter of his chewing.

What cold dream drove him across the bed?
What infection of the soul took hold his mouth?
Did his raw stumps strike sparks? Ignite
the scattered leaves of unsaid words across his tongue?

My hand hung frozen over him.
All the cities feared the metal scream
of my one father swallowing his teeth.

7.

It was three a.m., at least that late. The bus terminal was on a long unlit highway. It was so hot, your back slid across the seat on a cushion of grease. And the water was just poison. We pulled in for a Coke, to wash the tiny dust clods down our throats. The roof was made of vapor lights; it flickered, flickered; moths the size of doves battered up against the tubes. 2 Americans stood at the window, haggling over bus fare. Half of the place was a diner, darkened, on the far side of the room. A few tables, really, three stools at a counter. I stood staring. A kid sat at the table, in the shadows, grunting. He was lost in rolls of fat. Fat hung over the back of his t-shirt collar from his neck. His eyes were the size of beans, pushed deep in the slack yellow bulges of his face. I could hear his mouth work, these little wet sounds. He poured sugar into his fist from one of those table-top sugar dispensers with the slanted chrome top. You know them? He was pouring sugar into his fist like his fist was a coffee cup, filling his fist then tipping back his head—the lard welled up in a flat disk, the rings of Saturn clogging his pulse—and he poured the sugar in. Were those 2 at the counter his? Were they parents? With their backs turned, hunched against his grunts, his tiny eyes locked on my face, his small wet clicks. He licked the gravel off his lips. Stared. Stared at me. Little noises. Grunting. Pouring, pouring, swallowing, fist after fist, all night, abandoned.

Hello I said to him.
Brother!

8.

My father pale as a fingernail
drives demonic
across ghost-heavy night.

9.

So you're a man he said. *How much life does it take
to be a man* he said. *How much life.*

On a river bank
          tired
     women bent to meet their shadows.

       Stones
     pale as Easter eggs
staggered.

Someone laughed.

Sheets
      blew
            wide
                 as flags
                        in unexpected
          wind!

Back-
lit,
legs.
X-rayed.
Wide:
    arms held high:

              flight
                  on earth:
                     ecstatic
mundane.

Shirts, skirts, undershirts.
Diapers, bras, secret
      colored
      women
      things,

      thrown in
      scrubbed
      pounded:

                foam
                        launched
                itself:

        bubble tugboats, ice bergs, dragons
        went down
        through the village.

One radio crackled: Love
in cities never seen:
Canta y no llores, porque cantando
se alegran
                        Cielito Lindo
los corazones!

                        All that black hair
                        straight
                        down
                        their backs
over shoulders
                        writing
                        in
                                tri
                                        cate
stanzas across their necks.   Bare legs bruised purple.   Burned
summer dark.   Sweat

strung from throats to collarbones clear priceless beads
                                broke
their strings and hit
water
etched a codex

                                I daily
                                try

                        to decipher.

10

Hit it.

Drive mad across town, radio tuned
to sizzle-spit mariachi howls, drunken wide-hat wolves,
sixgun poets bawling pagan gospel of tequila
love
murder
ruin.
Six men in a Volkswagen, uncountable ghosts on the roof
    hung on for dear death, rubber burn on cobbles
    as we spun another corner, laughter's nasty
    calliope calling, dogbark
    midnight out skirts
of some flyspeck town,
cemetery next door
to the whorehouse, away
where the shouts and the shooting
and the trumpets and the shatter wake no one.
Grass shacks lined the compound where the women slept
with washtubs, t.v.'s, candy, photos, vinegar,
cigarettes, magazines, radios, memories, dreams,
chamber pots, underpants, razor blades, make-up,
bottles, babies, nightmares, and one bundle each
of rubber-band letters from some dreamboy who went
and never came home.

Dig the sign: CLUB VERDE PARA HOMBRES: CUELGEN SUS PISTOLAS.
Hang up your pistols, boys. Fat cops at the door
touched us all over, felt us for hardness under our clothes,
pulled from men's belts .38's, .44's, hung them
on pegs by the bar. Dark stench of toilets
let run from the stalls. Kneeling drunks
knelt at the bowls, penitent supplicants
to the Virgin of Filth. And inside—
shaky-legged tables
of tin—flaking stickers stuck
to our forearms, bright
paper freckles: TECATE

DOS EQUIS
CORONA
CARTA
BLANCA.

Homosexual bartender's long blue eyelids.

  Concrete dance floor stained
into maps of lost worlds
by beer spilled, by bootheels, by flat
women's sandals.
Black hair dyed orange
as cheap boots.
Black armpit feathers plastered with sweat.
In that corner, rock and roll:
the blind guitarist
followed the sounds
with his head, thin as sticks,
sang:

Old jou need es lob.

Love is all you need.
Love is all you need.
You can buy it here.
Unzip your hair, pull off your skin.
We watched them dance—farmhands
worked hard at having fun, the whores
  raised crops from them and pulled them
  off to harvest.
All those dresses
in the farmers' hands gone limp
wilted
by 1,000 palms.
We danced with them.
Love is all you need.

Around the room
cheap wooden doors
let light escape

in yellow stripes
from closetrooms
with 1 bed each, 1
light. 1 jug. 1 bowl.
1 woman.
1 filmy
sexy girlie thing
flung over the 1
wooden chair.
No exit.

I saw the crucifix above the bed, then her.

Cigarette burns tattooed her skinny arms.
Through an open door
I saw.
Love is all you need.
She dipped a knotted flower
rag into her bowl, ran water down her chest, her neck, her leg,
     then opening her thighs her other leg
       so tired it shook. I knew
that hair as thin as mist
uncurled from moistened flesh and rose.
She wiped her nodding breasts under her dress, washed off the heat,
washed off the weight from her brown ribs, washed off
     the smell, the feel, the
fingerprints.

And then looked up.

I smiled across the room, embarrassed rogue
through sheets of smoke.
Her stare burned my smile to ash.

You smile so easily, muchacho.
You think you offer me
condolences, or is this
business? Do you

think you understand?
      Love is all you need.
You'll never understand
until you lie here
ten or twenty nights
and think of home.
      Love is all you need.
You can spend money
to rest in me.
I'll carry you.
Would you carry me?
And if we meet at noon
      Love is all you need.
in the town plazuela,
you with your notebooks
and me with my flowers
always careful not to greet
anybody
      Love is all you need.
you will look away.
Ashamed at what you put here.

And I will walk away
out of town the long way
because the finest part of me you bought
was silence.
      Love is all you need.
Neither one looks back.
Then you go
but I remain
tomorrow
and tomorrow
and tomorrow.

Love is all you need.
Her lips were smeared, the color of crushed smiles.
I pointed to my mouth. She wiped her face. The knot
of cotton flowers cleaned her teeth.
We waved.

The blind guitarist shrieking in the corner.
The twisted Jesus writhing in His torture.
The brilliant coin cascade that hit her bed, a dark ranchero
    pushing in, she glanced at me, her hands
    at forehead, heart: sign of the cross. The closing door.
She loves you yeah, yeah, yeah.

11.

and he drives

I watch him

he drives

all fields burn black around him

his engine coughing sparks

fire skips

empty rivers

mummies twitch underground

he's laughing

I watch him

his engine coughing blood

flaming ravens hit the windshield

all those feathers

and he drives

and I watch.

12

Mi padre, muerto
ya por interminables años, no me deja
en paz: no se quiere ir: lo veo
cada día. Mi viejo se esconde
en los arboles, en el agua, en
las nubes de humo que huyen
de los cigarros de secretarias. O se mete
como ladrón
por mis ventanas
y me roba la comida. Es vivo: es capaz
de esconderse en la luna.
Y me dice,
    —Hijo, no queda nada.
     No queda nada.

Mi padre, sembrado
en su tierra Mejicana, echando retonos
en la pradera obscura del olvido, brilla:
cuando apago la luz, su cara
tira chispas en la esquina. Cuando
hago el amor, viene
corriendo. Cuando salgo
a la calle, me persigue
por los ojos
de niños callejeros.
Usa tacones de oro.
Me huele el café.
Lo veo
sin verlo.
Y me dice,
    —Hijo, no queda nada.
     No queda nada.

Mi padre, muerto ya y hecho polvo, llora
lagrimas de barro. Con voz de piedra me grita, me canta
su último consejo:

—Hijo, tu vida es una moneda.
Gástate bien. Porque
no queda nada.
No queda nada de mí.

13.

Now I know
what you tried to tell me:

the wind eats coyotes.

It'll swallow us too
who stand still long enough.
Even ore trains dense as stars
tumble in the desert wind:
engines flat-faced as vipers
disappear.

The wind eats the hills,
fossils fall to talc.

The far horizon folds up:
tumbleweeds carry off
our Mexico:
ten thousand miles of breath
collects beneath the moon,
coughs out our used-up names,
and stirs.

We can't escape the blow:
our prison bars
are memories,
are bones.

from *Many Mountains Moving*

JEAN VALENTINE

Tell Me, What Is the Soul

(Osip Mandelstam)

◊　◊　◊

There is a prison room,
the floor cement,
in the middle of the room
a black pool full of black water.
It leads to an invisible canal.
Plunder is the pool. Plunder is the canal.

By the wall,
by a fire,
he was reciting, in his yellow leather coat,
the thieves were listening, they offered him
bread and the canned stuff,
which he took . . .

from *The New Yorker*

Crazy Courage

◇ ◇ ◇

To Michael B.

Why do I think of Michael . . .
He came to my fiction class
as a man (dressed in men's
clothes); then he came

to my poetry class
as a woman (dressed in women's
clothes; but he was still
a man under the clothes).

Was I moved in the face of
such courage (man/woman
woman/man) . . .
Was I moved by the gentleness

of his masculinity; the strength
of his femininity . . .
His presence at the class poetry
reading, dressed in a miniskirt,

high boots, bright purple tights,
a scooped-neck blouse, carrying
a single, living, red rose, in a
vase, to the podium (the visitors,

not from the class, shocked—
the young, seen-it-all MTV crowd—
into silence as he's introduced,
"Michael . . .") And what it was, I think,

was his perfect dignity, the offering
of his living, red rose to the perceptive,
to the blind, to the amused, to the impressed,
to those who would kill him, and

to those who would love him.
And of course I remember the surprise
of his foamy breasts as we hugged
goodbye, his face blossomed

open, set apart, the pain of it,
the joy of it (the crazy courage
to be whole, as a rose is
whole, as a child is

whole before they're
punished for including
everything in their
innocence).

from *Prairie Schooner*

The Case

◊ ◊ ◊

Old wolf, I said,
leave a tatter
for my family:
a scrap, a rag,
a bone, a button—something
to bury.
　　　　Because, I said,
I've chased
the fast fox from
the henhouse, and twisted
the livid blossoms
from failing stems,
mercy, spare a rag,
a bone, a button,
for my family.

And because, I said, I sang
the names of saints
on Sunday, and lay
with another woman's
husband Monday eve, leave
a scrap, a rag,
a bone, a button—
to bury.

And he said:
It will take
whatever it is given. It will
be still.

from *The Paris Review*

DIANE WAKOSKI

The Butcher's Apron

◇   ◇   ◇

note: When I was a child, we lived in the midst of orange groves on Rus-
sell Street in East Whittier, California, just up the road from the
Nixon family grocery store, where I bought my popsicles from old
Mr. and Mrs. Nixon, father and mother of the late president. When
they expanded, adding a much bigger butcher's counter and a coffee
shop, their son Don Nixon, later featured in real estate scandals,
became the butcher.

—for Edward Allen

Red stains on the clean white bib,
the butcher's apron hanging
like an abstract expressionist painting
on the museum wall of my
childhood

—the most we ever ordered—
a pound of hamburger
to be fried in the black iron skillet
till the edges formed an ugly crust
like a scab on a skinned knee/
The art of the grill
was not found in our manless house.

The beauty of the red on the butcher's
white canvas, which occasionally streaked like an etching
across the white butcher paper
in which he wrapped the chuck, never translated
to the food eaten: grey meats

like steel wool, canned vegetables
with the colors of hospital walls,
sliced white bread like old often-washed
sheets and pillowcases.

My shock one day in the school cafeteria
to see Carol Gregory
    whose mother sewed her
    dresses as elegant as those in
    VOGUE magazine

unwrap a waxed paper packet of bright red
meat, in a puddle of something thin and dark/
to realize it was
Roast Beef,
the puddle
was beef blood! There in the Lowell School Cafeteria
I saw my first still life painting, beautiful and
different food among the Thermoses
of milk, the wax-wrapped peanut
butter or bologna sandwiches. Perhaps
I have added this detail:
    next to Carol's rare roast beef slices
    (she did not have a sandwich—just
    the meat) another piece of waxed paper on which
    was spread
        several spears of bright green
        asparagus.
Food eaten by the kids whose parents were rich
or had been to college
was different,
was like a painting?

My first-generation American mother grew up
in a house with a dirt floor, went to school
in a one-room schoolhouse. She drank German
coffee instead of milk
as a child. She lifted herself out
of North Dakota, became a bookkeeper
but never learned

about food, the telltale class
marking. In old age, she loves salty things like
Campbell's soups, frozen enchiladas in processed cheese sauce,
bacon white bread sandwiches and hates the nursing hospital
where they don't salt the food at all.

Plath imagined blood-red tulips in white hospitals
as I think of Georgia O'Keefe's poppies.
My mother who voted for Nixon and hates foreigners
dreams of those read and white cans
which might hold Chicken Noodle or Tomato
soups. She's never heard of Andy Warhol who
mimicked such cans, just as a butcher I talked to in our Michigan
supermarket said he had never eaten
shrimp or knew what people did with oxtails. His apron
too had the same bright red stains, not yet faded into
rust: crimson blood on canvas, the art
of childhood. Unhealed scars,
still capable of bleeding.

from *Many Mountains Moving*

Yellow Wolf Spirit

◇   ◇   ◇

It is the wolf running
across lightbeams that underscores
the powers of vision.
All else may fail out here on the road.
All else may become perilously a search
for meaning, in the way a theorist
can count only the yellow lines,
unable to learn the dark.

That wolf is meaning enough.
Its yellow spirit lopes across view;
the yellow lights sing to its iron coat.
What is learned from this witness
no book can attempt in words,
for the vision consecrates spirit
as the wolf runs through the heart.

Often we play out its maneuvers
admiring how wolfhair cloaks our intentions,
misreading instructions kindling the yellow eyes,
the music of its speaking.

Often, we become foul shouters and whistlers
or pursue careless quests of chaos to the woman
with the wolf's carpathian eyes
who would read us the cards.

From it we learned how to hunt and
invented the cunning of seduction,
the body language of stealth and
the lowered heads of pretentious desire.

Then it runs the dark through
our burnt out forests of identity, cajoling
our secrets and weakened essence
with its song, lyrics to the fear of
resonating sentience.

Wolf running, wolf songs.
We follow yellow wolf to edges of light
where the night world swallows its coat
and where its chest heaving resplendid
and strong drives the force of a lance
bolting with life.

from *Callaloo*

Run on a Warehouse

◇ ◇ ◇

What he had said came back to him.
Sectioned seat, sectioned seat.
The lift caught wind and swayed him in.
Big armoire, big armoire.

For some time he had felt it stir.
Sideboard door, sideboard door.
He sashayed through the conifers.
Dad's chair, dad's chair.

He had not known how far he'd come.
The blanket chest, the blanket chest.
A sourceless light suffused the run.
Love seat, love seat.

He had not come for his own sake.
All fixtures new, fixtures new.
Before the end he'd need to break.
Wall to wall, wall to wall.

So buckily he bore his load.
Filigreed frame, filigreed frame.
He could not see the lodge for snow.
Canopied bed, canopied bed.

He'll not forget the moment soon.
Cuckoo clock, cuckoo clock.
Now over snow a glimpse of moon.
Savvy desk, savvy desk.

There were but two things he required.
Glass breakfront, glass breakfront.
The slope was steep and he was tired.
Just a hutch, just a hutch.

from *The Paris Review*

Meeting Like This

◇   ◇   ◇

Ten years ago my brother sat firm
in a wheelchair on a logging road
to get in the way of a pickup truck.
(This was in the Kalmiopsis.)
Dave Foreman stood poised beside him.
The pickup gunned around my brother
but pushed Foreman back on his heels.
Back and back and back on a run
until he tripped and the truck braked
on top of him. The crew piled out
and called him a dirty Communist,
said he got his money from Russia.
Then the sheriff arrested Foreman
and let the crew, the law-abiding
road crew, pass.

Last week my brother hunkered
in the bow of an oar boat deep
in the shade of Hells Canyon.
(This was on the Snake River.)
Dave Foreman sat poised beside him.
Spring water ran high and strong,
and the boat flipped on the first class 5.
There in the rapid, the clashing boulders,
they both got wrapped in a loose line.
It almost drowned them, or maybe
saved them.

They enjoyed their reunion, they said.
It's okay to be run over by a river
on her way to work.

from *Weber Studies*

The Mill-Race

◇ ◇ ◇

Four-fifty. The palings of Trinity Church
Burying Ground, a few inches above the earth,
are sunk in green light. The low stones
like pale books knocked sideways. The bus so close to the curb
that brush-drops of ebony paint stand out wetly, the sunlight
seethes with vibrations, the sidewalks
on Whitehall shudder with subterranean tremors. Overhead, fain flickers

crackle down the window-paths: limpid telegraphy of the
late afternoon July thunderstorm unfurling over Manhattan.
Its set and luminous velocity, the long stalks of stormlight, and then the
        first drops
strike their light civic stripes on the pavement.
Between the palings, oat-panicles sift a few bright
grains to the stonecourse. Above it, at shoulder height,
a side door is flung open; a fire-exit; streaming from lobbies

come girls and women, black girls with ripples of cornrows and plaits,
ear-hoops, striped shadowy cotton-topped skirts, white girls in gauzy-
        toned nylons,
one girl with shocked-back ash hair, lightened eyebrows;
one face from Easter Island, mauve and granitic;
thigh on thigh, waist by waist; the elbow's curlicue and the fingers';
        elbow-work, heel-work,
are suddenly absorbed in the corduroyed black-rubber stairs of the bus.
        Humid
sighs, settlings, each face tilts up to the windows'
shadowless yards of mercuric green plateglass. In close-up

you can see it in the set and grain of each face,
despite the roped rainlight pouring in the bus-windows—
it's the strain of gravity itself, life-hours cut off and offered
to the voice that says, "Give me this day your
life, that is LABOR, and I'll give you back
one day, then another. For mine are the terms."
It's gravity, spilling in capillaries, cheek-tissue trembling
despite the makeup, the monograms, the mass-market designer scarves,
the army of private signs disowning the workplace and longing for night . . .

But this, at least, is the interspace. Like the slowing of some rural
water mill, a creaking and dipping pause
of black-splintered paddles, the irregularly
dappled off-lighting—bottle-green—the lucid slim sluice
falling back in a spittle-stream from the plank-edge. It won't take us
altogether, we say, the mill-race—it won't churn us up, altogether.
    We'll keep
this glib stretch of leisure-water, like our self's self—to reflect the sky.
But we won't (says the bus-rider, slumped, to herself). Nothing's
left over, really, from labor. They've taken it all for the mill-race.
    Even now,

as the driver flicks off the huge felt-edged wipers,
the rain slackening, lifting, labor
lengthens itself along Broadway. Fresh puddles
mirror in amber and crimson the night signs
that wit has set up to draw money: O'Donnell's,
Beirut Café, Yonah's Knish . . . People dart out from awnings.
The old man at the kiosk starts his late shift, whipping off rain-streaked
Lucite sheets from his new stacks of newsprint.

If there is leisure, bus-riders, it's not for you,
not between here and uptown or here and the Bronx. . . .
Outside Marine Midland, the black sea of unmarked corporate hire-cars
waits for the belated office-lights, the long rainy run to the exurbs.
Somewhere it may be, on a converted barn-roof in Connecticut,
leisure silvers the shingles, somewhere the densely packed
labor-mines running a half-mile down from the sky
to the Battery's bedrock rise, metamorphic, in water-gardens,
lichened windows where the lamp lights Thucydides or Gibbon.

It's not a water mill really, work. It's like the nocturnal
paper-mill pulverizing, crushing each fiber of rag into atoms,
or the smooth-lipped workhouse
treadmill, that wore down a London of doxies and sharps,
or the paper-mill, faërique, that raised the cathedrals and wore out hosts
   of dust-demons,
but it's mostly the miller's curse-gift, forgotten of God yet still grinding,
   the salt-
mill, that makes the sea, salt.

from *TriQuarterly*

Vespers

◇　◇　◇

Clarendon, Jamaica

Because it was a pilgrimage,
we left during the fifth hour of daylight
like the children in our textbooks

marching off to fight with devils.
Not yet women but no longer girls, my sisters and I
marched behind our mother to the river

where a secret society of women holding white sheets
waded into reflections of rose-apple blossoms,
into the icy, black morning water.

We watched our mother drowning sheets,
then men's shirts, her back bending, straightening,
her arms lifting the white cloth into the air,

a benediction, her arms as fluid as water,
as fluid as a Chancery *f* written in fresh ink.
I would pull the white shirts from the water

—embarrassed at touching my father, my uncles—
and drape them across rocks to bleach in the sunlight.
Walking home, arms filled with laundry

sweet with the smell of the sun now dissolving in the hills,
I would remember my mother in the dark water.
I would pray motherhood would never find me there.

from *The Southern Review*

Our Bird Aegis

◊ ◊ ◊

An immature black eagle walks assuredly
across a prairie meadow. He pauses in mid-step
with one talon over the wet snow to turn
around and see.

Imprinted in the tall grass behind him
are the shadows of his tracks,
claws instead of talons, the kind
that belong to a massive bear.
And he goes by that name:
Ma kwi so ta.

And so this aegis looms against the last
spring blizzard. We discover he's concerned
and the white feathers of his spotted hat
flicker, signalling this.

With outstretched wings he tests the sutures.
Even he is subject to physical wounds and human
tragedy, he tells us.

The eyes of the Bear-King radiate through
the thick, falling snow. He meditates the loss
of my younger brother—and by custom
suppresses his emotions.

from *Callaloo*

CONTRIBUTORS' NOTES AND COMMENTS

LATIF ASAD ABDULLAH (C-78059) was born in Oakland, California, in 1956. He is serving a twenty-two-year sentence for first-degree burglary at the Pelican Bay State Prison in Crescent City, California. His poem was published as part of the Pelican Bay Information Project.

Of "The Tombs," Abdullah writes: "In each soul there is a yearning that seeks to be compatible with the natural elements of creation. When the evil forces of the world create conditions of race hate, haves and have-nots, injustice, and environmental erosion, the soul will thus be plunged into an endless struggle to combat such evils. Poets arise out of all circumstances, bringing with them the suffering of oppressed souls, as well as the passions of compatible hearts. I rise from the suffering oppressed and bring with me their echoing voices. This poem was written out of that spirit, while in the bowels of the beast, observing empty souls that have been employed by the state, assigned as correctional officers."

SHERMAN ALEXIE was born in Spokane, Washington, in 1966. He is a Spokane/Coeur d'Alene Indian from Wellpinit, Washington, on the Spokane Indian Reservation. He is the author of a novel, *Reservation Blues* (Warner Books, 1996), and a short story collection, *The Lone Ranger and Tonto Fistfight in Heaven* (Harper Perennial, 1994), in addition to four collections of poetry: *Drums Like This* (Hanging Loose Press, 1996), *Old Shirts & New Skins* (UCLA American Indian Studies Press, 1993), *The Business of Fancy Dancing* (Hanging Loose, 1992), and *First Indian on the Moon* (Hanging Loose, 1993). His musical collaboration with Jim Boyd, *Reservation Blues—The Soundtrack,* was released on compact disc by Thunderwolf Records in 1995. A new novel, *Indian Killer,* will be published by Atlantic Monthly Press in spring 1997. The recipient of a 1992 National Endowment for the Arts Poetry Fellowship and a 1994 Lila Wallace–Readers Digest Writers' Award, Alexie lives in Seattle, Washington.

Of "Capital Punishment," Alexie writes: "I am a writer on *The Seattle Weekly,* the local independent newspaper, to which I usually contribute short opinion columns. In 1994 my editor at the *Weekly* suggested that I cover the execution of a child molester and murderer scheduled to take place at Walla Walla State Penitentiary here in Washington State. She thought a poet who was opposed to capital punishment might produce something original and thought-provoking. I accepted the assignment, had even packed my bags and arranged for interviews with local officials, when I changed my mind. I remembered the newspaper photograph, taken at a previous execution, of a young woman who wore a noose around her neck and carried a sign that read AN EYE FOR AN EYE. She looked like she was celebrating. That photograph frightened me. I realized that I was afraid of the aura of violence that must pervade such an evening. In short, I stayed away from the latest execution and watched the periodic news reports instead. The reporters told me what the condemned had eaten, what he said before they placed the noose around his neck, how his body looked after he died. Every little detail about the evening was reported, analyzed, and reiterated. I realized, despite my best efforts to hide, that I had witnessed a public execution. I realized that we all participate in these murders. I wrote the poem, 'Capital Punishment,' as a way of admitting my guilt and to call for the abolition of the death penalty."

MARGARET ATWOOD was born in Ottawa, Ontario, in 1939. She was educated at Victoria College, the University of Toronto, Radcliffe College, and Harvard University. She is the author of more than twenty-five books of poetry, fiction, and nonfiction. Her most recent novel is *The Robber Bride* (Doubleday, 1993); her most recent collection of poems, *Morning in the Burned House* (Houghton Mifflin, 1995). An alliterative children's book, *Princess Prunella and the Purple Peanut,* a paean to a particular letter, was published by Workman in 1995. Her other novels include *The Handmaid's Tale* (1985), which was adapted for the screen by Harold Pinter; the film was directed by Volker Schlondorff and released in 1990. Atwood has edited *The New Oxford Book of Canadian Verse in English* (1982), *The Best American Short Stories* (1989), and *The Oxford Book of Canadian Short Stories in English* (1986). She lives in Toronto, Canada, with her husband and daughter.

Of "Morning in the Burned House," Atwood writes, "This poem is about a small log house or cabin in northern Canada, which as a child I helped to build—I was a good log peeler and roofer—and which was struck by lightning, and burned to the ground, about seventeen years later. (That's why there are some ominous clouds beginning to appear in the poem). All of the objects named were in the house and were destroyed. So I suppose the poem is also about memory and time, and the way in which a thing can exist and not exist at the same time—and how different versions of the self can do the same."

THOMAS AVENA was born in Chicago in 1959. He received a 1995 American Book Award for editing and cowriting *Life Sentences: Writers, Artists, and AIDS* (Mercury House, 1994). Mr. Avena was the writer-in-residence and editor for "Project Face to Face," the AIDS oral history and arts project, during its installation at the Smithsonian Institution's Experimental Gallery. Known for his work on issues of treatment advocacy, he has addressed the National Institutes of Health and the Zurich AIDS Congress. In 1994, Mr. Avena was awarded both the International Humanitas Award for his work in AIDS education and the arts, and the Joseph Henry Jackson Award in literature for *Dream of Order* (Mercury House, 1996). He is coauthor with Adam Klein of *Jerome, After the Pageant* (Bastard Books/D.A.P., 1996), a monograph on the controversial paintings of Jerome Caja. Avena lives in San Francisco.

Of "Cancer Garden," Avena writes: "I wrote this poem because Ann Chamberlain, artist-in-residence at the UCSF Mt. Zion Cancer Center, asked me to read at the inauguration of the new garden there—one she designed in collaboration with the center's patients. I wanted this poem to evoke the experience of cancer in relation to time spent in this garden, which began as a windswept, concrete plaza, shaded by construction. I decided to write a personal poem that would also be appropriate to the inauguration of a public space, something I had done before, in 1991, at the Smithsonian Institution: 'another man tries living / anonymously // as / patches the color of radish / flower on his face // he continues / buying groceries // balancing the respirator // now / every line // every imprint / rendered colorless // becomes / common // common // common . . .'

"I wrote about the garden as a physical space, but also as a projection of the body and of the internal war—the extreme and bewildering processes—that the cancer patient is forced to undergo. I wanted these lines to flush and fill like the movement of blood within the body. Ann has said that 'Cancer Garden' distills the experience of people who pass through the garden. I don't know if this is true, but it contains part of my experience, of Ann's experience, and that of my life's partner—

William Lyon Strong (born William Shelton). Details from the poem are factual. Both Bill and I had been treated with vincristine, an alkaloid from the Madagascar periwinkle used against neoplastic tumors. Bill was 'the man whose veins collapsed nine times' during chemotherapy infusion. Ann and I are both cancer survivors, as was William, until his death, in October 1995, at the age of thirty-eight."

MARIE ANNHARTE BAKER was born in Winnipeg, Canada, in 1942. She is a member of the Little Saskatchewan First Nation, Saulteaux. As a graduate student in education technology at Gonzaga University, she studied the teaching of English and indigenous language using computers and multimedia approaches. She is the grandmother of two Okanagan girls, and her son, Forrest Funmaker, also writes poetry and performs. Her books include *Being on the Moon* (Polestar Books, 1990) and a chapbook, *Coyote Columbus Café* (Moonprint Press, 1994).

Baker writes: "In my contemporary storytelling performance piece, *Coyote Columbus Café,* the poem 'Porkskin Panorama' was an update on the love life of the 1990s First Nations woman. Simply put: 'more abuse.' The creative context of the poem was my attendance at the first gathering of North American Aboriginal writers held in Oklahoma in 1992. My disappointment in the event resulted from the overly academic display of the literary efforts of our people. Women writers, although some of the foremost writers on the continent, were still much in the background. However, the most telling thing for me was the absence of love poetry. 'Porkskin Panorama' is a type of love poem for the self. The poem helped me refire my spirit for writing as I bottomed out with more abject feelings about how so much First Nations literature was pretense and posture. Maybe my poem might be titled 'Driving the Wreck' if I dared to compare it with Adrienne Rich's 'Diving into the Wreck.' I, the persona, take one love (the love of porkskins) and then fool around (another name for love) with the nineties loves of casinos, powwows, and the voicing of culture as if in a diorama in a museum. The *Callaloo* version of the poem was edited to make it more 'bitchy' or 'whiny' in tone. The original is more strident and stabs into the false pride of the colonized native existence. Yes. We survived more than five hundred years of violence and abuse as women. Yes, we are going to survive whatever holocausts lie ahead, because even our pain is an aesthetic pleasure for us. Why deny the pain and rage because we don't want to appear 'angry' or 'bitter'? I celebrate my crabby days. Funny thing, at the most down-and-out emotional excess of my Oklahoma-to-South-Dakota-back-to-Manitoba trip, I conjured up two of my male mentors of the sixties, Clyde Warrior and Francis Kewaquedo. In spirit talk, I cried out how sad it was that they were not present. As sidekicks they had inspired me with their insight into the political workings and unworkings of our people. I felt reassured that I just had to work harder. They comforted me because of the generational difference in attitudes. This poem is my comeback or an inadvertent asking for a 'return of the gift.' I accept the *Callaloo* version as it was edited by First Nations women's influence, but I am saddened by our self-censure as First Nations writers. I prefer the published version of the poem in the *Coyote Columbus Café* chapbook. I especially loved the performance piece, where I actually grab a bullwhip out of my suitcase (labeled INDIAN BAG) and pace on the stage as a dominatrix. The awesome ripple of approval in the audience told me I was on to something. *Migwich* (thank you) to the Creatrix-Coyotrix spirit that has not been censored through the centuries."

SIDNEY BURRIS was born in Danville, Virginia, in 1953. He was educated at Duke University, the University of Vienna (Austria), and the University of Virginia. His book of poems, *A Day at the Races,* won the Utah Poetry Prize and was published in 1990. A book of criticism on the poetry of Seamus Heaney appeared in 1990 from Ohio University Press. He is working on a second manuscript of poems and a collection of essays on American and British poetry and culture. He teaches English at the University of Arkansas in Fayetteville.

Of "Strong's Winter," Burris writes: "Inasmuch as the poem concerns a young man who was my contemporary in a large high school in Danville, Virginia, I suppose it is fair to say that the emotional content of the poem has been simmering for a long time. Danville has been accurately and in some ways lamentably distinguished as the last capital of the Confederacy. The old capitol building, now a museum, was our public library during my childhood, and I used to spend hours reading under the images of fallen Southern soldiers. So prevalent was this association that many of my memories of the town have taken on the burnish of last things, things in their final stages. And this young man was no exception.

"I met him through my Latin classes at the high school. He was eccentric, rather tall and thin, dark-haired, pale-skinned, a committed loner; and throughout our class in Virgil, I never knew him to make a single mistake in his translations. His Latin grammar, both in composition and translation, was perfect. And in all of his classes he performed equally well, with an equal measure of mystery and aloofness. After graduation, he entered the army—this would have been 1971, a dangerous time to do such things—and soon thereafter turned up dead on the firing range. As I wrote the poem, various associations that I had formed overrode my sense of historical accuracy. But these associations have always represented for me the truth, if I might use that word, of this young man. Now I feel almost as if I should have been able to recognize that he was passing through his own final stage; I mean faced with the brooding presence of that old capitol building on West Main Street, how could I have done otherwise?"

ROSEMARY CATACALOS was born in St. Petersburg, Florida, in 1944, and was raised in San Antonio, Texas. Of Mexican and Greek descent, she is the author of two books of poetry: *As Long as It Takes,* a chapbook (Iguana Press, St. Louis, 1984), and *Again for the First Time* (Tooth of Time Books, Santa Fe, 1984). A former newspaper reporter and arts columnist, she was a Stegner Fellow in poetry at Stanford University from 1989 to 1991. At present, she is executive director of the Poetry Center and American Poetry Archives at San Francisco State University. She received a poetry fellowship in 1993 from the National Endowment for the Arts.

Of "David Talamántez on the Last Day of Second Grade," Catacalos writes: "David Talamántez is a composite of many Chicano children in many places and times. His educational experience is shamefully common and longstanding in the U.S., especially among the culturally and linguistically different. My parents, now in their seventies, as well as I and many of my friends, can recall incidents similar to David's in our own schooling. And just last month, a friend who writes on demographic and cultural diversity issues for a major Bay Area newspaper mentioned she was struck by how *current* David's situation is.

"Many of the specifics for this piece, for *this* representation of the Davids and the Dianas of our country, were drawn from a sheaf of notebook paper I found in 1988 on a school playground in my hometown of San Antonio, Texas. The exercises, the teacher's comments, even the child's written response on the 'rules' test, all are real. It was as if David (not his real name) had written the poem himself. And in a very true sense, he had.

"The form of the poem is one that asserts itself a lot recently, especially when I'm dealing with painful material. I like to think of the long lines as cantilevered, even precarious. The effort of maintaining their tension, balance, and integrity, and that of the stanzas, helps offset the emotional difficulty of making the poem.

"The piece is dedicated to Dr. José Angel Cárdenas, whose vision, scholarship, and leadership remain fundamental to the field of U.S. bilingual, bicultural education. ¡Que viva!"

MARILYN CHIN was born in Hong Kong in 1955. Her books include *The Phoenix Gone, The Terrace Empty* (Milkweed Editions, 1994), which won the 1994 PEN Josephine Miles Award, and *Dwarf Bamboo* (Greenfield Review Press, 1987). She was one of eighteen poets featured on Bill Moyers's PBS series *The Language of Life,* which aired in 1995. She teaches in the MFA program at San Diego State University.

Chin writes: "The poem 'Cauldron' was supposed to be shaped like a cauldron. The earlier version was fraught with stout handles and three legs, a literal replica of a sacrificial vessel in the Bronze Age. The image became abstracted in later versions for obvious reasons. The woman character in the poem is the true sacrificial vessel caught in the tides and vicissitudes of familial and global history."

WANDA COLEMAN was born in Los Angeles in 1946. Her books of poetry and fiction from Black Sparrow Press include *Imagoes* (1983), *Heavy Daughter Blues* (1987), *A War of Eyes and Other Stories* (1989), *African Sleeping Sickness* (1990), and *Hand Dance* (1992). A chapbook, *American Sonnets* (1-24) was published by Light & Dust Press in 1994. She has received a grant from the National Endowment for the Arts, a Guggenheim Fellowship in poetry, and a California Arts Council fellowship in fiction. She is currently working on a new manuscript. A poem by Coleman was selected by John Ashbery for *The Best American Poetry 1988.*

Of "American Sonnet (35)," Coleman writes: "Reversing negatives is a vital process integral to the survival of Americans of African descent, and I am no exception. When one critic attempted to demean my developing work, dismissing me as a 'jazz poet,' I decided to take that phrase and toot it as loud and long as possible. I vaguely conceived of a series of jazz sonnets in which I would bring together aspects of my heritages, the American and the African. It was circa 1976 and, while I was two years into my first breakthrough, I hadn't completely acquired the writing skills to pull off the task I set myself, although I boldly chased around for the requisite time and education. As it happened, I forgot my little project until the first American Sonnet sprang from my unconscious in 1986, ten years later. In this series of poems, I assume my role as fusionist, delight in challenging myself with artful language play. I mock, meditate, imitate, and transform, using any and every literary trick and device—even clichés—at will. Ever, beneath the off-rhyme, the jokey alliteration, and allusions, lurks the hurt-inspired rage of a soul mining her emotional Ituri."

JACQUELINE DASH was born in Jamaica in the West Indies in 1955. She has been a teacher and an accountant, and she is the mother of four. She is incarcerated in a women's prison, the Massachusetts Correctional Institute in Framingham. She studied in a workshop with the poet Rosanna Warren as part of a degree program administered by Boston University. She describes herself as a devout Catholic, whose goal is "to be a theologian and to finish the novel I am currently working on."

Dash writes: "In this poem, 'Me Again,' I am the custodian of my own pain. I want to leap out of myself—to let go of the pain. I want to forget—but instead I am back again to myself. My exterior self is not in command, it is my interior self who has taken command. In this poem the darkness of my life has overwhelmed me, yet the good days are not forgotten. This is a chastisement song of the dark turnings in my life. It seems that there is no light out of this darkness. It is closing in on me. I have to emerge from me again to my acceptable self."

INGRID DE KOK was born in South Africa in 1951. She attended the University of the Witwatersrand and the University of Cape Town before emigrating in 1977 to Canada, where she did an MA in English Literature at Queen's University in Kingston, Ontario. She is the director of extramural studies at the University of Cape Town. She has published a collection of poems, *Familiar Ground* (Ravan Press, 1988), has coedited a collection of essays on cultural freedom entitled *Spring is Rebellious* (Buchu Books, 1990), and was the guest editor of *World Literature Today's* 1996 issue on South African literature. Her poems have appeared in many anthologies, including Heinemann's 1995 *African Women's Poetry*. Her manuscript of new poems is provisionally entitled *Transfer*.

Of "Transfer," de Kok writes: "In 1990, after the unbanning of the African National Congress and other political organizations, a wave of exiles returned to South Africa. They returned to a country undergoing massive but uneven transformation. In the poem the collapse of my grandmother's house on the outskirts of Johannesburg reflects other ambiguities of change, and the poem explores the meaning of 'home,' belonging, the past and the future, under these new conditions."

WILLIAM DICKEY was born in Bellingham, Washington, in 1928, and grew up in the Pacific Northwest. He was educated at Reed College, Harvard University, and the University of Iowa Writers' Workshop. He was later a Fulbright Fellow at Jesus College, Oxford University. He wrote fifteen books of poetry, including *Of the Festivity,* which was chosen by W. H. Auden for the Yale Younger Poets Series in 1959; *More Under Saturn* (1963); *The Rainbow Grocery* (1978), which won the Juniper Prize; *King of the Golden River* (1986), which won the Bay Area Book Award; and *In the Dreaming: Selected Poems* (Arkansas, 1994). *The Education of Desire,* his last completed collection of poems, appeared posthumously from Wesleyan University Press in 1996. In the same year, Eastgate Systems, a software publisher in Massachusetts, published *The Complete Electronic Poems of William Dickey* as a two-volume set on diskette and CD-ROM. He died in San Francisco in 1994.

NANCY EIMERS was born in Chicago in 1954. She is the author of *Destroying Angel* (Wesleyan University Press, 1991) and has received the Discovery/*The Nation* Prize and a fellowship from the National Endowment for the Arts. She teaches at Western Michigan University and in the MFA program at Vermont College. She lives in Kalamazoo, Michigan, with her husband, the poet William Olsen.

Of "A History of Navigation," Eimers writes: "The poem began after a visit to the lighthouse museum in Whitehall, Michigan. I wanted to embed the rather dramatic narrative of a shipwreck, that of *Our Son,* one of the last Great Lakes sailing vessels, in a poem about a diner in Kalamazoo. Not surprisingly, the story of *Our Son* was too big and resisted me; the poem turned to something else. After numerous drafts, the shipwreck had disappeared from the poem, but the nautical folklore and imagery stayed along with a landlocked town and an argument and a diner decorated with smoke and fishing nets."

Of "A Night Without Stars," Eimers writes: "The setting of the poem is the fish hatchery outside of Kalamazoo, where we had driven to get away from the lights of town. We wanted to see the meteor shower, but the night was foggy, turning the streetlights into dandelion fuzz. Under a spell, the hatchery was achromatic and mute; our planet seemed to have misplaced its sky, and the poem came out as a spooked love poem."

MARTÍN ESPADA was born in Brooklyn, New York, in 1957. He has published five books of poetry, most recently *Imagine the Angels of Bread* (1996) and *City of Coughing and Dead Radiators* (1993), both from W. W. Norton. He is also the editor of the anthology *Poetry Like Bread: Poets of the Political Imagination* from Curbstone Press (1994). His awards include two fellowships from the National Endowment for the Arts, the PEN/Revson Fellowship, a Massachusetts Artists' Fellowship, and the Paterson Poetry Prize. A former tenant lawyer, Espada teaches in the English Department at the University of Massachusetts in Amherst.

Of "Sleeping on the Bus," Espada writes: "This is a poem about historical amnesia. Surely, not all of us have forgotten the Freedom Riders, but too often we forget the meaning of their legacy and fail to act in the spirit of that legacy. Rather, we become passive and distracted in the face of our own contemporary struggles. This is also a poem about who makes history. The anonymous 'brown man' in the third stanza is my father, from Puerto Rico, who was arrested in Biloxi, Mississippi, for not going to the back of the bus, and spent a week in jail. Even as I honor his solitary act of resistance, I realize that I do not fully appreciate that act. The bus metaphors arose from my acquaintance with bus travel; in fact, I began writing this poem on a Peter Pan bus."

Of "Rednecks," Espada writes: "In 1975, I worked at a Maryland gas station where the majority of customers came from white rural communities, and where the events described took place. The act of tenderness recounted in the poem shattered the 'redneck' stereotype of my imagination, and thus the use of that term in the title is my attempt to subvert the term. This brief incident compelled me to rethink my adolescent expectations: Who is truly ignorant? What is ugly? What is the cost of averting my eyes? Who are my teachers, and how do I recognize them? How do I act out of compassion? The poem endeavors to address these questions, still unresolved."

BETH ANN FENNELLY was born in Cranford, New Jersey, in 1971 and grew up in a suburb of Chicago. She did her undergraduate work at the University of Notre Dame and, after graduating in 1993, spent a year teaching English in the Czech Republic. She lived and worked in Karviná, a small coal-mining town on the Czech-Polish border. She is a teaching assistant at the University of Arkansas, where she is working toward her MFA in poetry. She has recently published poems in *Poetry Northwest, Another Chicago Magazine,* and *The Chattahoochee Review.*

Fennelly writes: "'Poem Not to Be Read at Your Wedding' was my first poem to appear in print. I had just moved down to Arkansas for graduate school and was really broke. My college roommate, Carmen Lund, was getting married and asked me to write her a poem for her wedding instead of giving a present. I wanted to, and I tried and tried, but at the time my parents were getting divorced after thirty years of marriage. I wondered how I could write an optimistic love poem knowing that two people could stick it out for thirty years and still have their marriage fall apart. It was out of this sense of despair that I wrote this sort of anti-poem. Poor Carmen never did receive a wedding gift."

ROBERT C. FUENTES (C-88749) was born in Corona, California, in 1958. He is currently serving a life sentence in California. He has been housed at the Pelican Bay State Prison in Crescent City, California, since its opening, and will remain so indefinitely ("until the Department of Corrections says otherwise"). "In This Place" was published as part of the Pelican Bay Information Project.

Of "In This Place," Fuentes writes: "The poem is an attempt to express the feelings of seclusion that prisoners who are incarcerated within the new-style security housing units (hole) live with everyday. In these modern-day cages, the prisoner has no access to the real world. All he possesses is his inner self, which he guards carefully, for there lies the strength that gets him by day by day. To show outwardly one is suffering in this place is to show that he is vulnerable when he cannot afford to be."

RAMÓN GARCÍA was born in Colima, Mexico, and grew up in Modesto, California. He graduated from the University of California, Santa Cruz, in 1991 and is currently working on his PhD dissertation in literature at the University of California, San Diego. His poems and short stories have appeared in a variety of journals and anthologies, including *New Chicano Writing, Quarry West, Outlook, Flight of the Eagle: Poetry on the U.S.–Mexican Border, The Americas Review, The Paterson Review, Poesida: Latino Poets Respond to AIDS,* and *Story.* He lives in Santa Ana, California, with his pet Siamese fighting fish Mowgli.

García writes: "'Salmo: Para El' is basically a parody of a poem by Marisela Norte entitled 'Salmo: Para Ella' from her CD collection

Norte Word; I see it as both a tribute and an offering to a poet I admire immensely. Norte's poem is a meditation on being a Latina, on existence as myth and stereotype. When I first heard her read this poem I was blown away. It seemed to me she had accurately described the search for another way of being, of existing. I had to respond. I felt that what she was describing was equally applicable to my own condition and personal predicaments."

SUZANNE GARDINIER was born in New Bedford, Massachusetts, in 1961. She is the author of the long poem *The New World* (University of Pittsburgh Press, 1993), a forthcoming book of essays called *A World That Will Hold All the People* in the University of Michigan Press's Poets on Poetry Series, and a manuscript of love poems called *Mercy*. She is at work on a novel entitled *The Seventh Generation*. She teaches at Sarah Lawrence College and lives in Manhattan. Her work appeared in *The Best American Poetry* in 1989 and 1990.

Of "Two Girls," Gardinier writes: "These two girls kept waking me up in the middle of the night in the last days of February 1995. I made these bent, broken sonnets for them, that they might be remembered in that year of terrible anniversaries, so we all might rest."

FRANK GASPAR was born in Provincetown, Massachusetts, in 1946. His first collection of poems, *The Holyoke* (Northeastern University Press) won the 1988 Morse Prize for Poetry. His second collection, *Mass for the Grace of a Happy Death* (Anhinga Press) won the 1994 Anhinga Poetry Prize. He received a fellowship in poetry from the National Endowment for the Arts in 1991. He lives in southern California and teaches at Long Beach City College. Gaspar's work has appeared in *The Georgia Review, Hudson Review, Sewanee Review,* and *Tampa Review.*

Of "Kapital," Gaspar writes: "This is a poem about the man who was my stepfather for about ten years. He was truly of the proletariat, a Portuguese laborer on the fish-wharves of Provincetown, Massachusetts, where I grew up. I was rummaging through Marx at the time I wrote the poem, and the vocabulary obviously carries over. Marx's elaborate theorizing belies—but just barely, I think—a great heart. Ideas are only important in human terms—in how they come to bear on our solitary and collective lives. There are several voices in this poem, speaking from the poems to the world, and from other worlds to the poem, so the stance is many stances. I hope something of this hard man's life shines here for a moment."

REGINALD GIBBONS was born in 1947 in Houston, Texas, and grew up just outside the city. A graduate of Princeton and Stanford, he edited *The Poet's Work* (Houghton Mifflin, 1979), an anthology comprising statements on poetics from such poets as Pessoa, Mandelstam, Pasternak, Lorca, Stevens, Seferis, Valéry, Crane, Auden, and Marianne Moore. *Roofs Voices Roads* (1979), his first poetry collection, won a prize from the *Quarterly Review of Literature*. Since 1981 he has been the editor of *TriQuarterly*. He teaches at Northwestern and in the low-residency MFA program at Warren Wilson College. The most recent of his four books of poems is *Maybe It Was So* (Chicago). A collection of short fiction, *Five Pears or Peaches,* appeared in 1991 (Broken Moon) and a novel, *Sweetbitter* (Penguin, 1996), won the Anisfield-Wolf Book Award and the Jesse Jones Award from the Texas Institute of Letters.

Of "White Beach," he writes, "I usually work from memory when I have sudden—and of course unexpected—access to what has already lain lost in forgetfulness for a while. I like to let memory choose unconsciously, this way, what is still alive in me emotionally, out of my own past history. When memories do return vividly, I'm close to thinking of them as potentially the elements of a poem when this return is not as a visual image of what happened in my own experience but as a phrase representing what happened—*words* that are part of my mental life *now,* representing something that happened *then.* (Asking myself how or why those particular words happen to be part of mental life now is another interesting part of the artistic process.) In January 1991, the following words came to me and I wrote them in my journal: 'Blown to a tatter by the wind / the cry of one gull or cat / and a lost child's cry / sound nearly the same.' I think what happened then was that I found myself remembering, in a vague way, having gone to the beach as a teenager—around 1964 or 1965. This meant driving with friends, starting beyond the northwest side of Houston (as its boundaries lay, at that time), then going through town and southeast toward the Gulf, and usually ending up at a beach at Freeport. About fifty miles, I think it was. I also recovered the thought of what had happened specifically on a couple of different occasions, and I began to write the poem not in order to *preserve* memories but in order to *use* them to get at what was also on my mind, night and day, as I was writing (as it often has been and is): the experience of racial identity in our country. So, teenage lust and love; and being out in the world together at seventeen; and accidents of harm; and both wanting and not wanting adult knowledge; and the danger and deep, soul-distorting pain, rage, and fear (on one side of the racial divide) and fear and false triumph (on the other) caused by racist attitudes, which are so completely mistaken and destructive—all that came into my poem. Plus the great pleasure, in and of itself, of writing and rewriting the lines to try to get the descriptions of everything just right."

C. S. GISCOMBE was born in 1950 in Dayton, Ohio. He attended SUNY Albany and Cornell University and was the editor of *Epoch* from 1983 to 1989. He is currently a professor of English at Illinois State University. His poetry books and chapbooks include *Postcards* (Ithaca House, 1977), *At Large* (St. Lazaire, 1989), *Here* (Dalkey Archive, 1994), and *Two Sections from Giscome Road* (Leave Books, 1995). He has received writing fellowships from the National Endowment for the Arts, the Fund for Poetry, and the Illinois Arts Council. A Fulbright Research Award from the Council for the International Exchange of Scholars allowed him to spend the first half of 1995 living and working in northern British Columbia. Works in progress include a book of travel essays, *Into & Out of Dislocation*; a poetry book in several sections, *Giscome Road*; and a mixed-genre book, an 'experimental biography' of the nineteenth-century Jamaican-Canadian miner and explorer John Robert Giscome.

Of "All (Facts, Stories, Chance)," Giscombe writes: "When I told my father that I'd had a poem selected for *The Best American Poetry,* he asked, 'On what subject?' It was a question that I'm not used to: it's quite reasonable, I think, but the language—and the straightforwardness—is from a different era. I'm more accustomed to yammering about composition, fields of reference, deferring closure, and 'What sorts of things does the poem do?' Subject? I surprised myself by stammering out that it was about painting. And then I added, 'And friendship and black culture and geography.'

"'All' is one of those poems in which culture and geography talk uncomfortably to one another (or try to). Or they talk *about* each other. I suppose I'm always drawn to the unlikeliest settings, to site-specific metaphors or visions occurring in 'wrong' places: in section one, for example, there's a reference to the "Midnight Special" song and myth, but I've moved it out of the South, out of funky Texas, and affixed the freedom-granting headlight to one of Amtrak's Empire Corridor trains, the Niagara Rainbow, as it drifts through Harlem toward the Canadian border at Niagara Falls. 'All' is the last in a group of three sequences about 'unlikely settings'—the first took place in the urban

South; the second was about the rough meeting places of urban, suburban, and rural in the Midwest. I'd meant for the entire group of poems to recapitulate and comment on, in some ways, the great migration, the journey north (which I've described elsewhere as 'the great geographic archetype'). The group of sequences ends in 'All' in upstate New York with my speaker-self looking on across Lake Ontario at the next (giant) step, the next country on the journey, Canada.

"Painting? (And friendship?) The poem began as a response to a poem written to me by my friend Ken McClane ('Song: a Motion of History' in his book *To Hear the River*); in that poem he evoked Henry Ossawa Tanner's famous *Banjo Lesson* painting, a work I've always found attractive and troublingly sentimental both. At the time I wrote 'All' I was much taken with the work of the black Hudson River School artist Robert Stuart Duncanson (whose *View of Cincinnati* is reproduced on the cover of my book *Here*), and early versions of the poem contained direct references to both Tanner and Duncanson. When my father asked me about the poem's subject I immediately thought of those two painters even though the references to them didn't survive into the final draft. Their presence is there, though: the boys outside Ken McClane's Omni are very Tanneresque; and very much about Duncanson and his landscapes are the poem's closing lines, '. . . soul's opaque & unbroken surface that looked // so smooth from far off, // unimaginably intricate at the thick lip.'"

KIMIKO HAHN was born in 1955 outside New York City. She is the author of the poetry collections *Air Pocket* (1989), and *Earshot* (1992), both from Hanging Loose Press, and *The Unbearable Heart* (Kaya Productions, 1995). Her prose has appeared in *BOMB* magazine and the anthology *Charlie Chan Is Dead* (Penguin, 1993). She was commissioned to write twelve portraits of "inspirational women" for the MTV special "Ain't Nuthin' but a She-Thing," which aired in November 1995. She is working on her fourth collection of poetry, *Volatile,* and a collection of prose, *The Downpour.* She has received fellowships from the National Endowment for the Arts and the New York Foundation for the Arts and was awarded the Theodore Roethke Poetry Prize in 1995. Hahn teaches creative writing and Asian-American literature at Queens College. She, her husband, and their two daughters live in Brooklyn.

Of "Possession: A Zuihitsu," Hahn writes: "Several years ago after a reading with Jack Hirschman, we sat at the Café Trieste talking about 'moribund capitalism,' poetry, my mother's death, his son's. Maybe Rilke. Maybe *The Tale of Genji*. He talked about studying 'possession,' in the sense of spiritual possession. Back on 105th Street I began to scribble. It may also have been on this trip that I read the *Wall Street Journal* articles cited in 'Possession.'

"During this time I was revising *The Unbearable Heart,* an elegiac manuscript. And I was writing more *zuihitsu* based on Sei Shonagon's *The Pillow Book*—except that mine are largely thematic collections. I reread poetic diaries by Ki no Tsurayuki, Basho, and Murasaki Shikibu with its equally exquisite annotations, Issa; also Kenko's *Essays in Idleness.* I liked the way prose paragraphs absorbed the contents differently than conventional poetry. The subject matter was allowed to be self-conscious. There is also an erratic quality to the *zuihitsu* that goes against chronology or any kind of logical progression. I could use my eye rather than my mind to arrange the paragraphs. A feeling of spontaneity. An anticlosure.

"In an attempt to move through my grief I returned to several long poems I'd been working on before my mother's sudden death. Political and outward-looking pieces. I found myself turning to newspaper clippings and other people's stories. And of course I brought in my own associations to subvert the diction or tone or attitude of those clippings and pin the *zuihitsu,* in this case, to my own pulse. Possess them."

GAIL HANLON was born in Boston, Massachusetts, in 1952. She grew up in the Pacific Northwest, received an MA from the University of Iowa, and now lives in Boston, where she works as an editor. Poems from her manuscript in progress have appeared in *Spoon River Poetry Review, Poet Lore,* and *Snail's Pace Review.* She received commendations in 1994 and 1995 from the National Poetry Competition, and "Plainsong" was awarded the National Writers Union Annual Poetry Prize in 1994.

Hanlon writes: "Although 'Plainsong' was written after a long period of thinking about the history of truthtelling, reclaiming authority, and the power of language, it took shape fairly quickly owing to the warm encouragement of Sharon Olds. While I very much wanted to write about these subjects I also resisted their disclosure, and that tension between revealing and concealing is at the center of the poem, influencing its form. The voice of the poem was, I think, the key to writing it; it seemed to acquire its own authority through the fusion of my history with that of historical and contemporary others."

HENRY HART was born in Torrington, Connecticut, in 1954. He is the author of one book of poems, *The Ghost Ship* (Blue Moon books, 1990), and has completed a second, *The Rooster Mask*. He has written three critical books: *The Poetry of Geoffrey Hill* (Southern Illinois University Press, 1986), *Seamus Heaney: Poet of Contrary Progressions* (Syracuse University Press, 1992), and *Robert Lowell and the Sublime* (Syracuse, 1995). From 1984 to 1995 he was the American editor of *Verse,* an international poetry journal; he is now the advisory editor. He teaches English at the college of William and Mary in Virginia.

Hart writes: "I started 'The Prisoner of Camau' in 1985 while teaching at the Citadel, the military college in South Carolina. I had read James Rowe's *Five Years to Freedom,* which gives an account of his years as a POW in Vietnam. I was particularly intrigued by what he said about surviving in solitude—how he kept his mind alive by constructing an imaginary *hacienda del sol* and by playing baseball on the back of a small tin cup. Having lived in England for seven years before going to the Citadel, I was also intrigued (and startled, to say the least) by my new environment. I heard stories about cadets who had gone to Vietnam, and of course my own life had been shaped by the Vietnam era. The narrative of 'The Prisoner of Camau' drew on these different sources, and originally was about twenty pages long. After writing several drafts, I realized it didn't work, put it away for about six years, and then around 1992 I exhumed it from my drawer and started revising it again."

WILLIAM HEYEN was born in Brooklyn, New York, in 1940, the son of German immigrants who subsequently moved to Suffolk County on Long Island. He is currently a professor of English and poet-in-residence at SUNY Brockport, his undergraduate alma mater, where he was a three-sport athlete and soccer All-American. He holds graduate degrees in English from Ohio University. A former Fulbright lecturer in American literature in Germany, he has won prizes and fellowships from the National Endowment for the Arts, the Guggenheim Foundation, and the American Academy and Institute of Arts and Letters. His books of poetry include *Depth of Field* (Louisiana State University Press, 1970), *The Swastika Poems* (Vanguard Press, 1977), *Long Island Light* (Vanguard Press, 1979), *The Chestnut Rain* (Ballantine, 1986), *Pterodactyl Rose: Poems of Ecology* (Time Being Books, 1991), *Ribbons: The Gulf War* (Time Being Books, 1991), and *The Host: Selected Poems 1965–1990* (Time Being Books, 1994). He is the editor of *The*

Generation of 2000: Contemporary American Poets (1984) and the author of a novel, *Vic Holyfield and the Class of 1957* (1986). In 1996, BOA Editions published his *Crazy Horse in Stillness,* a collection of more than four hundred poems.

Of "The Steadying," Heyen writes: "During the summer of 1992, not knowing what I was doing and usually in a state of semi-trance, I began to write what eventually became the several hundred poems now collected in *Crazy Horse in Stillness.* My book turns on the Great Plains, the buffalo, George Armstrong Custer and his wife, Elizabeth, the Battle of the Little Big Horn, and the Sioux warrior-mystic Crazy Horse, but its suffused subtext seems to me to be what might be called 'primal mind.' Again and again I seem to have hoped to enter and apprehend states of being beneath or beyond the usual welter of habits and details of my days. 'The Steadying,' written in a rush somewhere in the middle of all these poems, speeds through science, history, and personal experience, but its refrain stops the helter-skelter of associations and suggests (does it?) a necessary quieting. It may be that there is something frightening in the experience of writing hundreds of poems so fast, and of not feeling in control of time and place; in 'The Steadying,' I seem to be telling myself to dismount, to use my ammo economically. The tension in the poem, its swirl of vertigo against its balance of contemplation, is one I've felt since I wrote my first poem.

"As I read the newspapers and watch television now, as I live now, I don't know how else to keep, in Emily Dickinson's terms, the 'brain within its groove,' except by way of poetry. As she says, should even a splinter swerve, we're lost. Finishing poems like 'The Steadying,' I was found again, at least for a time."

JONATHAN JOHNSON was born in Fresno, California, in 1967. He received his MA from Northern Michigan University and is currently completing a PhD in English and creative writing at Western Michigan University, where he serves as poetry editor of *Third Coast.* He divides his remaining time between Marquette, Michigan, and the mountains of Northern Idaho, where he and his wife are building a small log cabin on the Johnson family farm.

Of "Renewal," he writes: "The town is Marquette in Michigan's Upper Penninsula. It's a remote place, a handful of lights between thousands of square miles of wilderness and the world's largest freshwater lake. Winters often last half the year, and the nearest big city is hundreds of miles south, so Marquette hasn't yet become a resort town. Lots of aspiring, broke artists have settled there, drawn as much by cheap rents as by the drama of Lake Superior and the woods. The poem's speaker is one of these artists, a painter (though I'm sure that's simply a way of writing about myself as a writer). When I started the poem I was primarily interested in his lethargy, how staring out of his high window at the snow had only made him feel more alone and desperate. As it turns out, the town becomes a kind of canvas, something he can claim and to which he can belong."

JANE KENYON was born in Ann Arbor, Michigan, in May 1947. She died of leukemia in New Hampshire on April 22, 1995. She had published four books of poems and a book of translations. Her poetry books, all from Graywolf, are *The Boat of Quiet Hours* (1986), *Let Evening Come* (1990), *Constance* (1993), and *Otherwise: New and Selected Poems* (1996). She had received fellowship grants from the National Endowment for the Arts and the Guggenheim Foundation. She lived with her husband, Donald Hall, on Eagle Pond Farm.

In "April, New Hampshire," an elegy published in *American Poetry Review,* Sharon Olds wrote:

> In their room,
> Don said, *This is it, this*
> is where we lived and died. To the center of the dark
> painted headboard—sleigh of beauty,
> sleigh of night—there was an angel affixed
> as if bound to it with her wings open.
> The bed spoke, as if to itself,
> it sang. The whole room sang,
> and the house, and the curve of the hill, like the curve
> between a throat and a shoulder, sang, in praising
> grief, and the earth, almost, rang,
> hollowed-out bell waiting for its tongue
> to be lowered in.

Speak, Memory is the book by Nabokov quoted in Jane Kenyon's "Reading Aloud to My Father."

Donald Hall writes: "Jane wrote many poems about her father's illness and death, of which 'Reading Aloud to My Father' is the latest and last. Reuel Kenyon died of cancer in Michigan in 1981; Jane and I stayed with him for much of his illness, helping Jane's mother care for him. When Jane was dying I thought of this poem. Music was her passion, as it was her father's; at the end, she could not bear to hear it, because it tied her to what she had to leave. In her last twenty-four hours, her hands remained outside the bedclothes, lightly clenched. I touched them from time to time, but I did not try to hold tight."

AUGUST KLEINZAHLER was born in Jersey City, New Jersey, in 1949. He is the author of seven collections of poetry, most recently *Red Sauce, Whiskey and Snow,* published by Farrar, Straus & Giroux in 1995. He has received a Guggenheim Fellowship and a three-year writer's award from the Lila Wallace–Reader's Digest Fund. He won a General Electric Award for Younger Writers in 1983 and the Bay Area Book Reviewers Award for poetry in 1985. He lives in San Francisco.

Kleinzahler writes: "'Two Canadian Landscapes' are of Montreal and Victoria, British Columbia, respectively. When I lived in Montreal in the late seventies the taverns were for men only, so I had Diana pay a call to one in the Greek district, near where I lived. The Pacific Northwest landscape actually consists of four poems I wrote in my twenties when I lived up there, poems I cannibalized and concertina'd into the one poem."

YUSEF KOMUNYAKAA was born in 1947 in Bogalusa, Louisiana. In 1969 and 1970 he served with the United States army in Vietnam. He was a correspondent and editor of *The Southern Cross.* Since 1985, he has taught creative writing and literature at Indiana University. He was the 1992 Holloway Lecturer at the University of California at Berkeley. His latest book, *Neon Vernacular,* was awarded the 1994 Pulitzer Prize and the Kingsley Tufts Award. He also received the 1994 William Faulkner Prize (Université de Rennes). His other books include *Copacetic* (1984), *I Apologize for the Eyes in My Head* (1986), *Dien Cai Dau* (1988), and *Magic City* (1992). He is a visiting professor at Washington University in St. Louis.

Of "Nude Study," Komunyakaa writes: "Images of black people have been caricatured worldwide, and such a global attitude of ridicule has been accepted as almost natural. Not only is it accepted as the norm by whites (and others), but blacks have often been programmed to accept this abuse. So, when I gazed upon John Singer Sargent's portrait of a black elevator operator, Thomas McKeller, the painting's grace and realism were striking. The golden-bronze had been brushed on the canvas with care: Thus, it wasn't hard for me to believe the two men had been friends, that McKeller had modeled for Sargent numerous times. What enraged me was to learn that the portrait had been unearthed in Sargent's studio after his death; it was hidden there because it embraced the true physical beauty of a black man. But what enraged me even more was to discover that McKeller's image had been cannibalized to depict Apollo and a bas-relief of Arion—other heads and hues grafted on to his classical physique. In fact, this can be viewed as a paradigm for the black man in Western culture. Hadn't his body been used to construct the economic foundation of America? Also, 'Nude Study' addresses the fear associated with the myth of black male sexual prowess."

STANLEY KUNITZ was born in Worcester, Massachusetts, in 1905. He discovered poetry at the local public library, and at age fourteen, when a teacher read Robert Herrick's poem "Upon Julia's Clothes," the boy raised his hand and said how much he liked *liquefaction* in "the liquefaction of her clothes." He attended Harvard. At thirty-seven, he was drafted into the army, where, declaring himself a pacifist, he cleaned latrines. After the war he received a Guggenheim Fellowship and taught at Bennington College. His first collection, *Selected Poems, 1928–1958,* won the Pulitzer Prize in 1959. He has also received the Bollingen Prize, the Brandeis Medal, the Lenore Marshall Prize, and the National Medal of Art presented at the White House by President Clinton in 1993. He was New York State's first official poet laureate. Other books include *The Poems of Stanley Kunitz: 1928–1978* (1979), *Next-to-Last Things* (1985), and *Passing Through: The Later Poems* (W. W. Norton), which received the National Book Award in 1995. He lives with his wife, the artist Elise Asher, in New York City and Provincetown, Massachusetts. "In youth, poems come to you out of the blue," Kunitz told Mary B. W. Tabor of *The New York Times* (Nov. 30, 1995). "They're delivered at your doorstep like the morning news. But at this age, one has to dig."

Kunitz writes: "I began writing 'Touch Me' in the midst of a furious late August storm on Cape Cod that marked for me the turning-point of summer and the conclusion of my eighth decade. The opening line is recalled from 'As Flowers Are,' a poem I wrote in the mid-fifties at the MacDowell Colony."

NATASHA LE BEL was born in New York City in 1977. A graduate of Saint Ann's School in Brooklyn Heights, New York, she is an undergraduate at Yale University, class of 1998. Her poems have appeared in *Hanging Loose*. She has studied drawing at the Rhode Island School of Design and at the Pont-Aven School of Art in Brittany, France. Her charcoal drawings were exhibited in 1995 at the Galérie de Gaugin in Pont-Aven. She won two Gold Key and three Silver Key medals in the 1994 Scholastic Art & Writing Awards. Both "Foot Fire Burn Dance" and "Boxing the Female" were written in her senior year of high school.

Of "Boxing the Female," Le Bel writes: "The woman in this poem is a figure in one of my charcoal drawings. She is much larger than I am. Her body is unnaturally bent inside a dense and silent space. Huge hands, thick hair, eyes shut, she presses against the boundaries of the ragged paper edges which enclose her giant shape. She is awkward and beautiful, on the verge of speaking. This woman is in the process of becoming herself, a direction in which I find myself constantly tumbling. Growing up in a four-generational family which has become predominantly a collection of women, I have always been given a strong sense of the feminine while an equivalent masculine element has remained, at times, a mystery. The woman in this poem is a reflection of all the women in my life who have given me the strength to break out of the boxes I have outgrown, to seek new spaces without walls or edges. Lovingly, I have dedicated the poem that grew from a drawing to Stefan, the man with whom I share my space and thoughts."

She also writes: "'Foot Fire Burn Dance' was written one night in my apartment in Brooklyn when I was struggling to think of one last poem that would complete my portfolio for Beth Bosworth's writing class at Saint Ann's. I had to force myself to write something, which is what made the poem turn out so loud and furious. It is about the crazy rhythms of the writing process; the way an idea sometimes has to be beaten out of the environment in order for it to be seized while it's still raw. It is about me and my very unladylike boots and the sounds I hear at night in my room and everything else that gets under my skin when I'm writing."

CAROLYN LEI-LANILAU was born in Honolulu, Hawai'i, in 1946. Her first book of poetry, *Wode Shuofa (My Way of Speaking)* (Tooth of Time, 1988) received an American Book Award in 1989. She recently completed her first book of essays, *Maloko Pu'uwai E Laka (Within Laka's Heart)*. She has lectured on translation and literary criticism in the

United States and China, particularly on *Nu Shu,* the Secret Women's Language from Hunan Province. She is the founder of Hale o Hawai'i Nei and director of *Ha'ina Mai ana Ka Puana (Tell the Story),* an oral history project that documents the historic relationship between *Kānaka* and native Californians.

Lei-Lanilau writes: " *'Kolohe* or Communication' is an example of my haunting slippery link with language(s). As a child growing up in Hawai'i, Carolyn Lei-Lanilau was fingerprinted and had to carry an identification card (which she still carries on her person today) that 'duly registered and identified [her] under the provisions of Act 246, Session Laws of Hawaii of 1947.' The consequences of being *Kānaka* (Native Hawaiian) and *Hakka* (a tribe in northern China that migrated south in the twelfth century, which over the years has been scandalously represented as the 'big feet, aggressive and fiercely independent women'), were both the traumatic and inspirational link in her deep interest with William Blake. As a baby, she was promised the moon by her cousin Stanley—and she fully expected to possess it. Years later, when she saw the engraving of Blake's ladder drawn to the moon with the caption 'I want I want,' she recognized herself—except that what she wanted was the ladder (of language) to bring her to earth. Not until 1993 when she curated an event at the Oakland Museum commemorating the one hundredth anniversary of the overthrow of Lili'uokalani, the last Hawaiian monarch, did she realize that it was finally safe to be *Kānaka.* Prior to this, she had, like many Hawaiians, *heard* Hawaiian but had been forbidden to speak Hawaiian. The irony was that all the words—and more—mentioned in this poem come from everyday speech. Names of streets and places, plants, birds, food, and other things were commonly uttered, but almost no one dared express themselves beyond one or two syllables in public. The language nearly became extinct.

"In the 1890s the missionaries and their descendants passed laws which prohibited *Kānaka* from *'Ōlelo o Hawai'i,* speaking Hawaiian. Only in 1987 did the Hawai'i legislature finally vote Hawaiian to be an official language. However, critical factors still endanger the lives of *Kānaka:* these include the fact that Hawaiian does not contain the verbs 'to have' or 'to be'; that the noun *writer* does not exist, because missionaries did not introduce *palapala* (paper, books, or anything printed) until the 1820s; and that Hawaiian is an oral tradition in which *Kānaka* enjoy hearing the beautiful sound(s) of the language sung and seeing it danced in *hula.* What compounds the dilemma is that *Kānaka* authors are not writing literature but are primarily addressing themselves to law, history, and the natural sciences. For at least twelve to fifteen years, there has been a steadily developing sovereignty movement in Hawai'i, which the tourist industry censors. In the realm of language, the rap group Sudden Rush and the beloved comedian Bu La'ia have been successful in raising the consciousness of island residents who would rather have sovereignty blow away with the winds in 'paradise.'

"Meanwhile, the literature on and about Hawai'i is being written by non-Hawaiians who have little or no knowledge of the Hawaiian metaphors that are so completely different from English ones; and who have no investment in the spiritual, emotional, and intellectual well-being of the *Kānaka*. Little literature written by non-Hawaiians features a *Kānaka* as a primary character and most does not even mention *Kānaka*. The paradisal landscape is always mentioned but never Hawaiian people.

"The irony of the lifelong process in which the author engaged herself in learning English, French, Latin, Mandarin and Hakka Chinese, and finally Hawaiian, is that her approach to all these languages—some of which were difficult to learn—was always stymied by her natural sense of syntax from the Hawaiian language that she did not speak. It is a shock and a fulfillment to her that she can finally speak (and possess) the language that is hers. '*Kolohe* or Communication' illustrates what a complex pleasure it is to embody many languages and cultures. As in all her work, a natural appreciation of sexuality is underscored by the work of William Blake and the *Kumulipo,* the Hawaiian Creation Chant, where in line six of the two thousand lines, the *Walewale* (*slime,* a nonpejorative euphemism for *sexual nutrients*) is mentioned."

VALERIE MARTÍNEZ was born in Santa Fe, New Mexico, in 1961. She grew up in Santa Fe, went to Vassar College, and received an MFA in poetry at the University of Arizona. After writing "It Is Not," she lived in Swaziland for three years, teaching English on a sugar plantation. What she misses most about southern Africa is a life where the visible and invisible weave themselves around and into us. Where her neighbors explained that a violent hailstorm resulted from the sudden and violent death of a "small man in the next village." Where bad "muthi" (spirit medicine), sprinkled over the playing field, contributed to her students' loss at netball. Martínez returned to Santa Fe in 1995.

Martínez writes; "'It Is Not' was written in a fit of heat in Tucson. A friend, new to the area, spent a day hiking, praying, and meditating in the Sonoran desert. The man she'd asked to pick her up at sunset spent the day agonizing over her safety, since the desert sometimes serves as a dumping place for the bodies of girls and women. I became inexplicably furious. The poem came to me on a hot, sleepless morning after Meagen arrived back home safely. I realized, after writing, that the desert has become what we have imposed on it. The speaker in the last stanza is unable to know the desert, so there is a staccato hesitancy not present in the first two stanzas, in which the characters have a clear grasp of what the desert means (or what they think it means). The speaker ultimately understands that there is no knowledge, no way to conceive of creation beyond human consumption."

DAVIS MCCOMBS was born in Louisville, Kentucky. Educated at Harvard (AB 1993) and the University of Virginia (MFA 1995), he is an editorial assistant at *Poetry* magazine. In 1993 he won the Ruth Lilly Poetry Fellowship. He has also received the Roger Conant Harch Prize and the Lloyd McKim Garrison Prize at Harvard. He lives in Chicago.

McCombs writes: "I grew up on top of the longest cave in the world. 'The River and Under the River' belongs in a series of poems about that cave and the regions known as the Caveland in south central Kentucky. I began the project after working two of my college summers as a ranger at Mammoth Cave National Park. It has occupied my writing almost exclusively in the three years since.

"I found this poem particularly difficult to write. Often I hear a poem's *music* (for lack of a better term) before I've written a word of it. Here just the opposite occurred: the words all came, in draft after draft, months before I discovered the rhythms holding them together.

"Carlos is my great uncle, Carlos McCombs, who drowned in the Green River near Brownsville, Kentucky, in September 1908."

SANDRA MCPHERSON was born in San Jose, California, in 1943. She is the author of eight collections of poems, including *The Spaces Between Birds: Mother/Daughter Poems 1967–1995* (Wesleyan University Press, 1996), *Edge Effect: Trails and Portrayals* (Wesleyan University Press, 1996), *The God of Indeterminacy* (Illinois, 1993), *Streamers* (Ecco, 1988), and *The Year of Our Birth* (Ecco, 1978), which was nominated for a National Book Award. She is a professor of English at the University of California at Davis and has also taught at the University of Iowa. She has received two Ingram Merrill Foundation grants, three fellowships from the National Endowment for the Arts, an award from the American Academy and Institute of Arts and Letters, and a Guggenheim Fellowship. She was recently featured in a segment of *The Language of Life* with Bill Moyers. She has one daughter, Phoebe, and is married to the poet Walter Pavlich.

McPherson writes: "'Edge Effect' took at least two years to write and maybe as many as four. I'd held the epigraph in mind before the truly complementary subject presented itself. For some time I'd been researching two subjects that seemed somehow to touch, different but relatable: self-taught artists making their way however clumsily through visual images that captivated them, and trails making their way under the sometimes graceless foot through natural grandeur and nature-made particulars. 'Edge Effect' was to be the poem that most explicitly linked these two worlds.

"Walking a strip of Oregon beach, I was surprised by a sudden 'gallery' of stacked stones along the wave-worn rocks against the cliff. I asked a local person about this phenomenon, and he said the creations started a year or two before and are always anonymous, intentionally created in secret. The works implicitly invited passersby to create their own balanced stone towers or steeples or bodies.

"This was 'outsider' art and it was outside. But it needed to collaborate with waves, sea creatures, birds, beachcombings, physics, the moon, and it was only a few feet away from a force that would demolish it eventually.

"The principle of edge effect seems to recommend a choice: not of the simpler centers of individual communities but of richer meeting places. Gods and humanity, birds and underwater breathers, a noble mineral world and sentient changeability, the lush and the stark, softness and hardness, childhood and layers of maturity.

"Somehow my father-in-law, George Pavlich, now eighty-two, a weight-lifter who for half a century has been a friend of Jack LaLanne, had to have a place in these encounters and creations. Maybe it was partly because his weight room is so stark and clean and purposeful, and yet the human body that changes form in the weight room is warm-blooded, laborious and dissatisfied, humid, ambitious, and visionary.

"I concluded by imagining that the edges leave their safe, too 'pure' centers and choose each other."

JAMES MERRILL (1926–1995) was born in New York City. He was the son of the financier Charles Merrill, the founder of the giant brokerage firm Merrill Lynch, and his second wife, Hellen Ingram. He interrupted his studies at Amherst College to serve in the infantry for a year during World War II. Returning to Amherst, he impressed his professor, Reuben Brower, with his analysis of the relation of rhetoric to emotion in the writings of Marcel Proust. He graduated summa cum laude, spent a year teaching at Bard College, then went to Europe, to Paris and Venice mostly, for a two-and-a-half-year journey of self-discovery. This is the subject of Merrill's memoir, *A Different Person* (1993). *First Poems* came out in 1951, *The Country of a Thousand Years of Peace* eight years later. Already in these elegantly crafted poems, Merrill pursued visions of angelic transcendence. "There are moments when speech is but a mouth pressed / Lightly and humbly against the angel's hand," he wrote in "A Dedication." He used sonnets as narrative building blocks in poems determined "to make some kind of house / Out of the life lived, out of the love spent," as he put it in *Water Street* (1962), his watershed volume. In such poems as "A Tenancy" and "An Urban Convalescence," he developed the relaxed conversational style that he perfected in *Nights and Days* (1966), *The Fire Screen* (1969), and *Braving the Elements* (1972). Sometimes dismissed as an opera-loving aesthete, Merrill was able to identify himself with history and could handle subjects that defeat most poets (the anarchist's bomb, the space traveler's capsule, the shopping mall, and the alcoholic's recovery program). He had grown up in a Manhattan brownstone blown up by a radical fringe group in 1970. In "18 West 11th Street" he writes about that incident, as if his own life were passing before him in the slow-motion replay of the blast. His books received two National Book Awards, the Pulitzer Prize, and the Bollingen Prize. The epic poem begun in *Divine Comedies* (1976) and extended in two subsequent volumes was published in its entirety as *The Changing Light at Sandover* (1983), which won the National Book Critics Circle Award. His most recent books of poetry are *Late Settings* (Atheneum, 1985), *The Inner Room* (Knopf, 1988) and *A Scattering of Salts* (Knopf, 1995). *Recitative,* a collection of Merrill's critical prose edited by J. D. McClatchy, appeared from North Point Press in 1986. Merrill owned homes in Stonington, Connecticut, and New York City, and spent many winters in Key West, Florida. He died Monday, February 6, 1995, while on holiday in Tucson, Arizona.

W. S. MERWIN was born in New York City in 1927, and grew up in Union City, New Jersey, and in Scranton, Pennsylvania. From 1949 to 1951 he worked as a tutor in France, Portugal, and Majorca, and later earned his living by translating from French, Spanish, Latin, and Portuguese. He has also lived in England and in Mexico. *A Mask for Janus,* his first book of poems, was chosen by W. H. Auden as the 1952 volume in the Yale Series of Younger Poets. Subsequent volumes include *The Moving Target* (1963), *The Compass Flower* (1977), and *The Rain in the Trees* (Knopf, 1988). *The Carrier of Ladders* (1970) won the Pulitzer Prize. He has translated *The Poem of the Cid* and *The Song of Roland,* and his *Selected Translations 1948–1968* won the PEN Translation Prize for 1968. In 1987 he received the Governor's Award for Literature of the State of Hawaii. *The Vixen,* his latest collection of poems, appeared from Knopf in 1996. Other recent books are *The Lost Upland* (1992, Knopf), about France, and *The Second Four Books* (Copper Canyon Press, 1996), poems. He was the first recipient of the Dorothy Tanning Prize from the Academy of American Poets in 1994. Later that year he won a three-year writer's award from the Lila Wallace–Reader's Digest Fund. He lives in Hawaii—in a place called Haiku, on the island of Maui.

Of "Lament for the Makers," Merwin writes: "The title and form are a deliberate allusion, of course, to a poem by Chaucer's Scottish contemporary, William Dunbar."

JANE MILLER was born in New York City in 1949 and currently lives in Tucson, where she is on the creative writing faculty at the University of Arizona. She is the author of *Memory at These Speeds: New and Selected Poems* (Copper Canyon Press, 1996), *Working Time: Essays on Poetry, Culture, and Travel* (University of Michigan, 1992), and several earlier volumes of poetry, including *August Zero* (1987) and *American Odalisque* (1993), both also from Copper Canyon. She has received a Lila Wallace–Reader's Digest Writers Award, a Guggenheim Fellowship, and two grants from the National Endowment for the Arts.

Of "Far Away," she writes: "After my father's death, my brother and I had to choose a coffin and then try to maintain our composure through his burial and the official mourning period—a week during which, according to Jewish law, the family sits on wooden boxes, suffering physically as well as emotionally, out of respect for the dead. None of this tradition need be understood by the reader, as I hope the poem is carried along by its lyrical lament. My father worked most of his life, even as a boy, sharing first with his parents and then with his own family whatever he had. This seems poetic to me; that is, spiritually alert. By extension, his generosity reminds me that poetry regards the unheralded and dispossessed."

SUSAN MITCHELL grew up in New York City and has lived in Province-town, Chicago, Washington, D.C., Paris, and Rome. She is the Mary Blossom Lee Professor at Florida Atlantic University and lives in Boca Raton. Her most recent book, *Rapture* (HarperCollins, 1992), won the first Kingsley Tufts Award and was a National Book Award finalist. *The Water Inside the Water,* an earlier collection, was published by Wesleyan University Press in 1983. She has received grants from the Guggenheim and Lannan Foundations and from the National Endowment for the Arts. Her translation of Canto 21 of Dante's *Inferno* is forthcoming in Norton's *Treasury of World Poetry,* and excerpts from her notebooks have just appeared in Norton's *The Poet's Notebook.* She is at work on her third book of poems and a book of essays to be published by HarperCollins.

Mitchell writes: "Though many of my poems simply erupt, complete surprises to me, there are others that accumulate gradually out of images, fragments of lines, shadowy glimpses on the far side of language. Still others, after an initial outpouring, refuse to go any further for the longest time. 'Girl Tearing Up Her Face' goes back to some journal jottings dated July 1983. Under the heading '3 Photos of Myself,' there are the titles of three projected poems:

1. Girl on a Swing
2. Girl with Cherokee
3. The Banyon Tree

After this list comes the first draft of 'Girl Tearing Up Her Face' in the form of a prose poem. Why did it take me twelve years to finish? I had wanted to get the other two portraits or photos into rough draft before I started to revise 'Girl on a Swing,' but I was unable to write 'Girl with Cherokee.' It was too painful. What I had to deal with was a photo that my mother had taken of me and a man in his late forties, a member of the Cherokee tribe living on the Cherokee reservation in North Carolina. This was back in the fifties, and I must have been about eleven. All through my childhood I had been obsessed with Native American culture, and my father thought that he was giving me something that I wanted when he pressed a fifty-cent piece into the hand of the man who stands beside me in the photo. Even without the photo, I can remember the man's left arm reaching across my back and coming to rest on my own arm. My words for that gesture now would be glib, automatic, sold-out. What I had wanted was for him to throw the fifty cents on the ground and refuse to pose, and if he did pose, to stand stiffly aloof from me so that I could feel the electric charge of his fury. My face exudes that blankness I know so well from many students when they don't want to give a clue to what they are feeling. Perhaps the man's accepting smile is his version of this. Perhaps he was thinking of something else. As for my parents, I found out years later that they forced themselves to go through with this only because they thought it would make me happy. In a way, they, too, were coerced, all four of us were, though by very different forces. So maybe the photo should be titled, 'Hey, This Is Ridiculous! What Are We Doing Here?' For some reason, I thought I needed to be able to say what I have written here before I could go on with 'Girl on a Swing,' the poem that became 'Girl Tearing Up Her Face.'

"It took me time to find the right point of view for this poem. In the rough draft, I speak through the voice of the girl in the photo. I needed to separate from her, needed to split so that I could talk about and interact with her. It's that relationship with its peculiar mix of sexuality and aggression that emerges from the bits and pieces of the torn-up photo.

"And 'Girl with Cherokee,' would I write it now as a poem? What might get me into that poem would be unanswered questions about coercion and love, knowledge and pretense and their effect on language. What is the price that language would have to pay?"

PAT MORA was born in El Paso, Texas, in 1942. She writes poetry, nonfiction, and children's books. Her four poetry collections are *Agua Santa: Holy Water* (Beacon, 1995), *Communion* (Arte Público, 1991), *Borders* (Arte Público, 1986), and *Chants* (Arte Público, 1984). In 1994, she received a poetry fellowship from the National Endowment for the Arts, and in 1986, a Kellogg National Leadership Fellowship. A former university administrator, she is now a freelance writer and speaker living in Cincinnati. She is completing a book of family memories, *Voices from the Garden: Voces del jardín.*

Of "Mangos y limones," Mora writes: "A woman I am privileged to know from El Salvador told me casually one day about her last pregnancy, her son swelling in her as her teenaged daughters watched, cringed. A laughing survivor of life's injustices, this woman, who is a housekeeper in California, speaks only Spanish and is full of spunk. 'Mangos y limones' is part of my poetry collection *Agua Santa: Holy Water.*"

ALICE NOTLEY was born in Bisbee, Arizona, in 1945, and grew up in Needles, California. She was educated at Barnard College and at the

Writers' Workshop at the University of Iowa. During the late 1960s and early 1970s she led a peripatetic poet's life (San Francisco, Bolinas, London, Essex, Chicago) before settling on New York's Lower East Side. She was married to the poet Ted Berrigan. She has written more than twenty books of poetry and has twice received poetry fellowships from the National Endowment for the Arts. Her *Selected Poems* appeared in 1993. *The Descent of Alette,* a book-length poem, was published by Viking Penguin in the spring of 1996. She now lives permanently in Paris with her husband, the British poet Douglas Oliver.

Notley writes: "'One of the Longest Times' is from a manuscript called *Mysteries of Small Houses,* a book of autobiographical poems about the nature of the self and the persistence of its identity over time. In writing these poems I practiced an informal self-hypnosis in order to get in touch with the basic self in which my past is suspended. This particular poem was hard to achieve (some came remarkably quickly); I remembered the event but not clearly and finally had to imagine it rather than re-live it. It was written after almost all the other poems, so it 'knows' the whole book."

NAOMI SHIHAB NYE was born in St. Louis in 1952. She has worked as a visiting writer in schools for twenty-one years. She currently lives, writes, and edits anthologies in San Antonio, Texas. Volumes of poetry include *Red Suitcase* (BOA, 1994) and *Words Under the Words: Selected Poems* (Far Corner Books/Eight Mountain Press, 1995). She has a collection of essays, *Never in a Hurry* (University of South Carolina Press, 1996). She is also the author of books for young readers: *Sitti's Secrets, Beñito's Dream Bottle, This Same Sky, The Tree Is Older than You Are,* and *I Feel a Little Jumpy Around You,* coedited with Paul Janeczko, all available from Simon & Schuster.

Nye writes: "'The Small Vases from Hebron' was written the day of the massacre of praying Palestinians in their local mosque by an Israeli terrorist. But the newspapers, at least in my town, didn't call him a terrorist. One story even described him as a 'good doctor.'

"As I drafted my usual angry letter to the editor, my eyes fell onto the quiet congregation of miniature flower vases in the center of our wooden table. I'd carried them home in my hand luggage after a recent visit with our Palestinian relatives in the West Bank. The town of Hebron is famous for its glass.

"The vases weren't crying. They weren't cracked. Since when have objects been wiser than people? All day in my grief and rage I tried to enter them, to become a simple vessel. But I kept thinking about the children of Hebron growing up with their complicated legacies of long oppression and loss—could anything feel simple to them anymore? What would they do with their anger? Would it take the place of all the flowers they might have otherwise carried? I thought of my grandmother, who, when asked at the age of 105 what she thought about the 'peace process,' answered bluntly, 'I never lost my peace inside.' She was luckier than many."

ALICIA OSTRIKER was born in New York City in 1937. She is a professor of English at Rutgers University. Her books of poetry include *Songs: A Book of Poems* (Holt, Rinehart and Winston, 1969), *Once More out of Darkness and Other Poems* (Berkeley Poets' Press, 1974), *A Dream of Springtime: Poems 1970–78* (Smith/Horizon Press, 1979), *The Mother/Child Papers* (Momentum Press, 1980), *A Woman under the Surface* (Princeton University Press, 1982), *The Imaginary Lover* (Pittsburgh, 1986), *Green Age* (Pittsburgh University Press, 1989), and *The Nakedness of the Fathers: Biblical Visions and Revisions* (Rutgers University Press, 1994). Her critical and scholarly works include *Writing Like a Woman* (University of Michigan Press) and *Stealing the Language: The Emergence of Women's Poetry in America* (Beacon, 1986).

Ostriker writes: "I have just hunted through old notebooks to find the first draft of 'The Eighth and Thirteenth.' The poem was begun in May 1991, during a week I spent alone on our family's land in the Berkshire backwoods, half a year after I'd had a mastectomy. It was a time of healing and pleasure, a space of solitude that produced a torrent of writing—some of it about the surgery, and some of it about dancing, swimming, flowers, mushrooms, art, history, friendship. Notes from books I was reading. Random scribbles. One evening in the middle of that week I was finishing dinner, sipping wine, when the public radio station I listen to up there—the Five College Radio Network out of Amherst—played Shostakovich's Eighth Symphony, which I had never heard before. I wrote while listening, and afterward. The siege of Leningrad during World War II is memorialized in the Eighth Symphony; the massacre of the Jewish population of Kiev is memorialized in Shostakovich's Thirteenth. The quotations from the composer's notebook may be found in his *Autobiography,* a book of ferocious, brilliant prose, which will tell you just what it was like to survive as an artist under Stalin. I read the *Autobiography* while revising the poem. For a while there was a passage, later cut, about Plato's cave as the sewage tunnel of history. For a while there was a section on Dr. Mengele at Auschwitz. And for a while I had, as an epigraph, two lines from Margaret Atwood: 'The facts of this world seen clearly/are seen through tears.' I am not sure where I came across the quotation from Marina Tsvetaeva, the great Russian poet who committed suicide in exile. Friends have told me that the literal version of what she said is simpler and harsher: 'Poets are Yids.' Tsvetaeva was herself a pure Russian, not a Jew. 'Never again' is a post-Holocaust slogan—flying in the face of our knowledge that genocide of one kind or another occurs again and again in human history. One mourns, one hopes."

RAYMOND PATTERSON was born in Harlem, New York, in 1929. He is the author of *26 Ways of Looking at a Black Man and Other Poems* (Award Books, 1968), *Elemental Blues* (Cross-Cultural Communications, 1983), and a recent opera libretto, *David Walker,* written with support from a National Endowment for the Arts Collaborative Fellowship. He taught for many years in the English department at the City College of New York and is a trustee of the Walt Whitman Birthplace on Long Island, where he lives with his family.

Patterson writes: "Begun as a simple listing of losses, 'Harlem Suite' waited almost a decade to find its true subject, the creative strength of a community. Section Three refers to a walk along 125th Street, a main commercial artery in Harlem."

CARL PHILLIPS was born in Washington in 1959 and grew up on air force bases. A classics major at Harvard, he taught high school Latin for nearly a decade. His first book of poems, *In the Blood* (Northeastern University Press), was selected by Rachel Hadas for the 1992 Samuel French Morse Poetry Prize. A second volume, *Cortège,* was published by Graywolf Press in the fall of 1995. A visiting professor in English and American Literature and Language at Harvard last year, he teaches creative writing, English, and African-American literature at Washington University in St. Louis. His work appeared in *The Best American Poetry* in both 1994 and 1995.

Of "As From a Quiver of Arrows," Phillips writes: "The poem began from spending a bleak St. Louis afternoon alone and deciding to pick up around the bedroom. In the course of gathering the usual items—dirty clothes, stray pens, an old hairbrush, etc.—it occurred to me how suddenly valuable the items belonging to one's lover, were he to die, would become. A piece of clothing, for example, could at any

273

moment be elevated to a kind of relic—secular and, to my ways of thinking, sacred, too. I suppose this started a train of thought regarding devotion—to the beloved, to the body, to the dead—which in turn triggered a vague memory of the Roman emperor Hadrian's devotion to (and elaborate treatment of the dead body of) the boy Antinous, as described in Marguerite Yourcenar's novel *The Memoirs of Hadrian*. The rest is the poem, a series of questions for which I find no suitable answers and, accordingly, offer none."

WANG PING was born in Shanghai in 1957 and came to New York in 1985. Her poems have appeared in *The World, Sulfur, Chicago Review, Talisman, West Coast, River City,* and *The Best American Poetry 1993*. Her book of short stories, *American Visa*, was published by Coffee House Press in 1995, and a novel, *Foreign Devil*, appeared from the same publisher in 1996. She is editing and translating an anthology of Chinese avant-garde poetry, 1982–1992. She lives in New York City.

Of "Song of Calling Souls," Wang Ping writes: "That hot afternoon in April 1994, after reading at William Paterson College in New Jersey, I suddenly had an urge to visit the cemetery where the six unclaimed bodies from the *Golden Venture* were buried. I didn't know the cemetery's name, but something told me it was nearby. I went to the library, took out all of the March issues of *The New York Times,* and found the article on these unfortunate people. They were buried in Rosemary Cemetery, not far from William Paterson. It seemed easy to get there, and my friend who drove me had years of professional training in reading maps. But we kept getting lost. Every time we thought we had found the cemetery, we turned out to be wrong. When we finally got close to our destination, a thunderstorm came down with such force and fury that we had to pull over to the side of the highway and wait. By the time it stopped, it was already past five, and the cemetery had just closed.

"I returned home perturbed. Day and night, I saw the six drowned faces. They had wanted me to visit them but, at the last moment, had blocked me. Perhaps they felt ashamed? There's nothing worse for a Chinese than to become a *yie qui*—a stray ghost, someone who dies and is buried away from his or her homeland. They wanted me to do something for them, and the only thing I could do was to write, to call their names and help their spirits find their way home. For a whole week, I sat at my desk, living their hope, struggle, despair, and loss. My mind followed them from the Fijian mountains to the bottom of the *Golden*

Venture to the common grave in Rosemary Cemetery. 'Song of Calling Souls' is my prayer for the six unclaimed dead in New Jersey. May their spirits find peace and home. When I finally finished the poem and staggered into the sun, half-blind from exhaustion, it suddenly occurred to me that there are still hundreds of people in detention centers all over America, thousands slaving their lives away for the minimum salaries to pay off their debts, and thousands more waiting for an opportunity to sail across the Pacific for a great dream. Can I call all of their names?"

STERLING PLUMPP writes of himself: "I was born January 30, 1940, on a cotton plantation in Clinton, Mississippi. I was reared by my maternal grandparents, Victor and Mattie Emmanuel, who passed away in 1955 and 1993 respectively. I am the father of Harriet Nzinga, a junior at DePauw University in Greencastle, Indiana. Currently I am a professor in the departments of English and African-American Studies at the University of Illinois at Chicago. I am divorced or rather a single father. I have traveled once to Australia and twice to South Africa." He is the author of two collections of poems, *Johannesburg and Other Poems* (1993) and *Blues: The Story Always Untold* (1989), both from Another Chicago Press. *Home/Bass* will be published in 1996. Plumpp was a coeditor of *TriQuarterly* #69 and editor of *Somehow We Survive,* a collection of South African poetry and fiction (Thunder's Mouth Press, 1982).

Of "Two Poems," Plumpp writes: "'Poet' concerns itself with the birth of Thebe Neruda Kgositsile, born February 24, 1994. He is the son of Keorapetse Kgositsile, a major South African poet, and his wife, Cheryl Harris, a professor of law at Kent College in Chicago and currently a visiting professor at UCLA Law School. The poem celebrates the birth of Thebe as well as the birth of a new South Africa with majority rule, which became effective in 1994. Within 'Poet' are the names of personalities and events from the 'long road' of liberation to majority rule in South Africa.

"'When Spirit Spray Paints Sky' is about Keorapetse Kgositsile, a friend of near three decades who contributed greatly to the Black Arts Movement of the 1960s. He literally erases the barriers between African and African-American. He is at once a revolutionary and a lover of blues and jazz. He achieves the status of 'hero' by exhibiting the 'real' in African and African-American life. Considerable bounce came into his steps with his marriage to Cheryl Harris and the birth of Thebe Neruda. His latest works are *To the Bitter End* (Third World

Press, 1995) and *When The Clouds Clear* (COSAW Publishing, South Africa)."

KATHERINE ALICE POWER was born in Denver, Colorado, in 1949. She is currently incarcerated at the Massachusetts Correctional Institute in Framingham. As an antiwar radical in September 1970, she committed herself to revolutionary action and was implicated in a bank robbery in which a beloved Boston policeman was killed. In Corvallis, Oregon, in September 1993, a successful restaurateur named Alice Metzinger surrendered herself as the fugitive Katherine Power and was sentenced to prison on October 6, 1993. She had, as Lucinda Franks wrote in *The New Yorker* (June 13, 1994), remained on the FBI's "Ten Most Wanted" list longer than any other woman in American history. "A high-school valedictorian from a devout Catholic family, Power had been transformed seemingly overnight from a sedate Brandeis coed into an armed felon," Franks wrote. While other fugitives were captured, she "managed to create within Oregon's New Age culture a protected life that seemed carved from the American dream." But if to some she remained "an emblem of the lost idealism of the sixties," others were less forgiving. "The woman who left Oregon last fall was praised, lionized, and wept over, and the woman who was then arraigned in Massachusetts was as strongly derided and condemned," Franks wrote. "The return of the fugitive had brought long-buried strife to the surface, however briefly, reminding Americans that the wounds of Vietnam remained unhealed."

Power notes that the terms of her twenty-year probation (which she is serving concurrently with her eight-to-twelve year sentence) prohibit her from profiting from the publication of any work related to her crime or her years in hiding. Since she is unwilling to censor from her work "references to such events as the Vietnam War, such acts as committing crimes for political purposes, or such ideas as the powerful necessity of nonviolence," she does not accept money for her writing. The conditions of her probation are under appeal to the U.S. Supreme Court.

Of "Sestina for Jaime," Power writes: "The primal themes of love and separation, and the flow of rivers and solidity of rocks, need a poetic form as firmly defined as the natural laws of physics and biology. The sestina form requires a sustained look at the relationships among the elements whose names are used for the end-words of the lines: *years, river, cold, rock, summer,* and *house."* Jaime is the name of Power's son.

REYNOLDS PRICE was born in Macon, North Carolina, in 1933. Educated in the public schools of his native state, he earned an AB summa cum laude from Duke University. In 1955 he traveled as a Rhodes Scholar to Merton College at Oxford University to study English literature. After three years and the B Litt degree, he returned to Duke, where he continues teaching as the James B. Duke Professor of English. Since the appearance of his first novel, *A Long and Happy Life,* in 1962, he has published more than twenty-five volumes of fiction, plays, essays, and translations. *A Palpable God* (1978) provided translations from the Old and New Testaments, with an essay on the origins and aims of narrative. His novel *Kate Vaiden* won the National Book Critics Circle Award in 1986. His three volumes of poetry are *Vital Provisions, The Laws of Ice,* and *The Use of Fire.* He is a member of the American Academy of Arts and Letters, and his work has appeared in sixteen languages. In 1997 Scribner will publish his *Collected Poems.*

Price writes: "'Twenty-One Years' is one of the many diary poems which I've written for an ongoing sequence called *Days and Nights.* In mid-life I began to deplore the fact that, since I'd never kept a successful journal, many striking aspects of my daily life were vanishing fast. In 1983, then, I began writing generally brief, spontaneous, and quickly finished poems which memorialized some fleeting aspect of my immediate life. More than a hundred poems have gathered in the ensuing years; and while I've worked to make them accessible to most readers, the poems can also recall for me certain fugitive moments that remain, in part, private. As a reader, I've always enjoyed such poems by others; and 'Twenty-One Years' is a clear example of my attempt to write a poem that can satisfy at least two audiences—me and the world."

ALBERTO ALVARO RÍOS was born in Nogales, Arizona, in 1952. He is the author of seven books and chapbooks of poetry and two collections of short stories. His most recent books are *Pig Cookies* (Chronicle Books, 1995) and *Teodoro Luna's Two Kisses* (Norton, 1990). He has received the Walt Whitman Award and a Guggenheim Fellowship. He is Regents' Professor at Arizona State University, where he teaches creative writing and literature.

Of "Domingo Limón," Ríos writes: "Domingo Limón, a friend of mine since childhood, met an untimely death that was cruelly foreshadowed as in a bad novel.

"A week before our tenth high school reunion, the local newspaper erroneously reported Domingo Limón's death. It came to our attention because one does not forget a name like his. When we showed up at the reunion, so did he, and the event occasioned as much laughter as nostalgia.

"Not a week after the reunion, however, Domingo suffered a serious health crisis and, incredibly, he died. There was no warning, no prior condition, nothing but the event of the week before."

PATTIANN ROGERS was born in Joplin, Missouri, in 1940, and graduated Phi Beta Kappa from the University of Missouri in 1961. She received her MA from the University of Houston in 1981. She teaches in the creative writing program at the University of Arkansas during spring semesters. She is the mother of two grown sons and lives with her husband in Colorado. Her sixth book, *Firekeeper: New and Selected Poems,* was published by Milkweed Editions. It was one of five finalists for the Lenore Marshall award in 1994. She has received two grants from the National Endowment for the Arts, a Guggenheim Fellowship, and a poetry fellowship from the Lannan Foundation. Her five previous books are *The Expectations of Light* (Princeton University Press, 1981); *The Tattooed Lady in the Garden* (Wesleyan University Press, 1986); *Legendary Performance* (Ion Press, 1987); *Splitting and Binding* (Wesleyan, 1989), and *Geocentric* (Gibbs Smith, 1993).

Of "Abundance and Satisfaction," Rogers writes: "I'm not certain how this poem came about. I suppose its beginning was similar to the origin of most of my poems—a feeling of form, a vague pattern of intuition.

"The poem comes into being as I attempt to bring that pattern to realization by asking questions of it, by filling it with detail, hopefully discovering its subtleties and nuances, its quirks and inconsistencies, its energy, as the language creates and reveals them.

"Where is the place of this particular detail within this intuition?

"And where does this specific possibility fit inside this form?

"And suppose this were the weather and this were the time and these were the circumstances—within this pattern, what then?

"What is abundance? What is satisfaction? What is the nature of my ongoing engagement here?

"Riotous, indestructible, enigmatic clarity. That angel."

QUENTIN ROWAN was born in New York City in 1976. He attended Quaker schools in Brooklyn and Manhattan and studied poetry writing with Cathy Bowman at Bennington College at a summer work-shop. He was the editor of his high school literary magazine. He currently attends Oberlin College, where he is majoring in English and plays in various rock-and-roll bands.

Rowan writes: "I wrote 'Prometheus at Coney Island' in my junior year of high school, 1993. I guess I wanted Prometheus to meet with the modern world in a sort of hotbed of urban and cultural decay, a place that had once flourished, where reenactments of the Civil War would take place on large open lawns, yet today makes one feel hollow and nostalgic. There is an emphasis on taste, sight, and touch, because Coney Island is a smorgasbord of these sensations, and taste, sight, and touch are things that have not changed with the passing of time."

DAVID SHAPIRO was born in Newark, New Jersey, in 1947. Since 1965, he has published many volumes of poetry, art criticism and translation, including an early monograph on John Ashbery's poetry, the first book on Jasper Johns's drawings, and a pioneering text on Mondrian's flower studies. He graduated from Columbia College in 1968 and spent two years at Clare College, Cambridge, as a Kellett Fellow. He received the 1977 Zabel Prize from the National Academy and Institute of Arts and Letters as well as grants from the National Endowment for the Humanities, the National Endowment for the Arts, and the Ingram Merrill Foundation. He has taught at numerous universities, including Columbia and Princeton, and is currently a professor of art history at William Paterson College and an adjunct visiting professor at the Cooper Union. He is also on the faculty at Bard College's Milton Avery School of Arts. Recent books include *After a Lost Original* (1994) and *House (Blown Apart)* (1988), both from Overlook. In 1971 his book *A Man Holding an Acoustic Panel* was short-listed for the National Book Award in poetry.

Shapiro writes: "The scientific vision charms and revolts me, and I appropriate its banal vocabulary sometimes. I admire the real rope in Picasso and the fictional slice. Thus, I have used physics textbooks, language primers, mistranslations—all tones like paint from the tube. This poem is an homage to my friend, the painter Gregory Botts, whose work I was pleased to introduce to the critic Harold Bloom. The pun in the title emerges from the German and the invocation to Bloom's book, *The American Religion,* for which Botts's paintings of 1990 *Autumn: The Night* serves as cover. The painter's imagery of sunflower and heroic land are retraced in this poem. What I admire in

Botts's work, here and elsewhere, is his intransigent urge to marry fig- ure, flower, and the fatal geometry of nature. This late romanticism warns us to beware of poets who would reduce their art to pietistic sto- ries in regularity or the equally canonic debris of discontinuity. Poetry should be, as in our best painting, abstract and figurative at once and always. Starting from *The New York Times*'s "Science" page and its neu- tral conversation about death and its noises, I tried to orchestrate some- thing large and late for a sequence about the dying of an American dream and its peculiar anti-sublime. I call these adventures "the tradi- tion of American darkness." I have dedicated this poem to the memory of my mother, Fraida Chagy, who had a wild love of justice and pro- found hate of racism and anti-Semitism. Four other remarks are embedded in this poem, moreover. Francesco Clemente responded swiftly and negatively when asked about the influence of dream on his art. Jeremy Gilbert-Rolfe crushed wittily some playful spirit by assert- ing that art was exactly *not* a game. Annie Plumb wittily observed that Gregory's picture *Autumn* might become a flag for a new nation. My son, early a pantheist, remarked that God's birthday was every day and infinity a little word. The Hebrew pun on Adam as red clay balances the title's melancholy, I hope, and celebrates my agreement with de Kooning that paint was invented to represent the flesh. And poetry, to represent desire."

ANGELA SHAW was born in Denville, New Jersey, in 1967, and spent her childhood in West Virginia. A graduate of Swathmore College, she received an MFA from Cornell University, where she has taught for the past three years. She lives in Ithaca, New York.

Of "Crepuscule," Shaw writes: "For a time after reading William Matthews's 'Mood Indigo' I wanted all poems to begin, as that one does, 'from the porch,' a place that is both home and not-home, an uneasy intersection of public and private life. In writing 'Crepuscule' I knew only that I wanted this woman to walk out of her house, to smoke a cigarette, to rest on the porch a while. For some months I struggled to get her there. Ultimately, I think, she gets away from me, outstripping my wishes at the end of the poem. She continues to be my elusive subject."

REGINALD SHEPHERD was born in New York City in 1963 and raised in the Bronx. He received his BA from Bennington College in 1988 and MFA degrees from Brown University (1991) and the University of

Iowa (1993). His book *Some Are Drowning* (Pittsburgh) was chosen by Carolyn Forché for the 1993 Associated Writing Programs' Award Series in Poetry. His second collection, *Angel, Interrupted,* will appear from Pittsburgh in 1996. He is the recipient of a 1993 Discovery/*The Nation* Prize, a 1993 Paumanok Poetry Award, the 1994–95 Amy Lowell Poetry Travelling Scholarship, the 1994 George Kent Prize from *Poetry,* and a 1995 fellowship from the National Endowment for the Arts. Shepherd's work appeared in the 1995 edition of *The Best American Poetry.* He lives in Chicago and teaches at Northern Illinois University.

Shepherd writes: "'Skin Trade' is fairly straightforward about its procedures and concerns. It's more directly topical than most of my poems in its approach to the complex of matters gathered under the rubric of race, but that material is not the entire matter of the poem. In my work as a whole, as in my life, the ghostly presence of 'race' is never quite exorcised. As Frantz Fanon wrote, 'The Negro is not. Any more than the white man.' But race is a phantasm whose effects are real. What we make of what we are made is a test presented to all in this society. I hope that having been produced (and having produced myself) as a black person (that is, as a contradiction in terms) permits me to make Fanon's prayer my own: 'O my body, make of me always a man who questions!'"

ENID SHOMER was born in Washington, D.C., in 1954. Her books are *Stalking the Florida Panther* (1988), winner of the Word Works' Washington Prize, and *This Close to the Earth* (University of Arkansas Press, 1992). A new collection of poems, *Black Drum,* is forthcoming in 1997. Her first book of fiction, *Imaginary Men* (University of Iowa Press, 1993) won both the Iowa Short Fiction Prize and the *Southern Review*/LSU Fiction Award given annually for the best first collection by an American author. Shomer has received grants from National Endowment for the Arts and the Florida Arts Council. She has lived in Florida most of her life, but for the last four years has spent half of each year in New York City. In 1994, she was writer-in-residence at the Thurber House.

Of "Passive Resistance," Shomer writes: "Several months before the trip to Las Vegas that spawned 'Passive Resistance' I was rereading Edna St. Vincent Millay and was struck again by the powerful 'Dirge without Music,' especially its form. I decided to model a poem on it, alternating rhyming quatrains of eight-beat lines with quatrains of pentameter. The eight-beat line turned out to be the right vehicle for so much narrative detail combined with emotional intensity. Much as I tried, however, I was unable to incorporate the shorter stanzas, so my poem is all eight-beat lines in a simple rhyming pattern.

"Some of the most ironic facts didn't fit in the poem. I was put up in the only hotel in Las Vegas without a casino (not even a slot machine!). The purpose of my poetry workshops was to help the Nevada Desert witnesses express their feelings about atomic testing, but some were too angry to write anything but invective. (Among the participants was a fellow who had thrown a pie in Ronald Reagan's face on camera.) Perhaps the greatest irony of all was that after more than a decade of arranging a private caravan into the desert, the organizers learned that the government provided free bus tours of the atomic test site. So that is how we went—on a big, bouncy bus."

GARY SOTO was born in 1952 in Fresno, California, the heart of the San Joaquin Valley. Everyone in his family was a field or factory worker. His father packed boxes at the Sunmaid Raisin Company and his mother peeled potatoes for Redi-Spuds. When Gary was five, his father died in an industrial accident. Inspired by Donald Allen's *New American Poetry* anthology, he took up poetry. He graduated from California State University in 1974 and went on to take an MFA from the University of California at Irvine two years later. He is the author of twenty-one books, including *New and Selected Poems* (Chronicle Books, 1995), which was a finalist for both the Los Angeles Times Book Prize and the National Book Award. In 1990 his *Baseball in April* was recognized as the American Library Association's "Best Book for Young Adults." His other books include *Jesse* (Harcourt Brace, 1994). Forthcoming titles are *Junior College* (Chronicle Books) and *Buried Onions,* both due in 1997. He edited the spring 1995 issue of *Ploughshares.*

Of "Fair Trade," Soto writes: "When we were first married, my wife, Carolyn, and I took over my brother's cottage apartment, which was near downtown Fresno, in an area where winos, newly arrived immigrants, gap-toothed bikers, and prototypes of the first homeless people scraped by. We took over my brother's problems. Since I didn't have a job, I reread Bachelard's *Poetics of Space,* a smart-alecky French text that in graduate school sounded wiser than the Bible. Later, though, as I tried to assemble a life with my wife, in a place that we could call our own and, thus, build up memories together, I could have called consumer fraud on that philosopher. What we needed was not poetic gibberish about houses, such as they were, but paint and new windows in that neighborhood. The place was insane, and our neighbors insane, especially Ziggy, a crusty remnant of another era and patron of the *barrio* bar called The Space. One day, when Ziggy called me to look at something in his apartment, I said, 'OK, let's kill some minutes,' and followed him into his cottage and right to his kitchen. Giggling, he grumbled a spacey warning and then stomped the linoleum floor in some crazy hoedown. From underneath the refrigerator, a legion of cockroaches of every age swarmed from hiding, swarmed and took new positions under the stove and in the broom closet. What is this, I thought, momentarily frightened. Ziggy had thrown back his head and laughed at his little joke. He stomped the floor again, and the cockroaches swarmed again, taking new positions. Alas, it was Ziggy entertaining his guest as well as he could toward the end of his life.

"In spite of the area, I did my best to entertain my wife. One Sunday I took her down to the Eagle Café ['Azteca' in the poem], just two blocks away but watery in the distance of summer heat and yellowish vapor. Everything had quieted to hangovers and deeper levels of boredom. Ignorant me, I ordered fried chicken smothered in a lava-like run of canned mushroom sauce. My wife may have had a tuna salad; I'm not sure. Dripping with sweat, I realized that I had ordered a meal meant for a wintery day. That Sunday outing would have been forgotten, except I witnessed an exchange that was not right—the waitress taking advantage of a *campesino* who had come in to buy bread. The waitress told him that they didn't sell bread, just toast, and I guess the man wanted it badly enough to order it to go. But when he was asked to pay, the number of an ancient cash register jumping up with a *ching-ching,* I could see his shock that the two pieces of toast—neither of them buttered or jammed or even presented on a paper plate—cost sixty-five cents. Right there, I witnessed pride, for he hesitated but knew he had only one choice. He paid and left, the bell jingling on the door. After I paid for our meal, I looked for the line of crumbs this man might have left for me to follow."

JEAN STARR was born in Alexandria, Virginia, in 1935. Both her parents were Cherokee. She studied journalism and history at Franklin College, and for many years she taught English and ethnic studies at American Legion High School, an inner-city alternative school in Oak Park, California. She was the first director of the American Indian Education Program for her school district and a former officer for the National Education Association's American Indian/Alaskan Native Caucus. Her books include *Songs of Power* (Little Sister Publications, 1987) and *Tales from the Cherokee Hills* (John F. Blair Publishing, 1988). She died in 1994. She is survived by her husband, Winn.

Of "Flight," Winn Starr writes: "In July 1974, Jean was a delegate to the National Education Association convention in Chicago. One evening, she went with some friends to see O'Hare, the world's busiest airport. She told me of how she stood by the fence around the runways, watching in fascination as the lights of the planes sped down the runways, arced into the dark sky, and vanished in the distance. As she watched, she wondered where the people were going; what they would do; and if they would return. This was the genesis of 'Flight.'"

DEBORAH STEIN was born in New York City in 1977. She attended Hunter College High School in New York City and studied fiction and poetry at the University of Virginia's Young Writers' Workshop. In the fall of 1996, she will enter her sophomore year at Swarthmore College, where she is concentrating in women's studies and theater. She has won an award for her work from the City College High School Poetry Festival.

Of "heat," Stein writes: "I wrote this poem when I was in the eleventh grade. My creative writing teacher said my voice was absent from it—instead, she wanted to hear about my own thoughts and experiences. Looking at it now, I don't think that was fair—I'm definitely there, watching and observing, trying to carve out my own space. I guess that's always been where I've felt most comfortable."

ROBERTO TEJADA was born in Los Angeles in 1964. He currently lives and works in Mexico City, where he edits *Mandorla,* an annual journal in English and Spanish of advanced poetry and poetics from the Americas. His writings on contemporary Latin American artists and photographers have appeared in numerous catalogs, as well as in *Third Text* (United Kingdom) and *Arte Internacional* (Colombia). He has published reviews in the *Village Voice Literary Supplement.* His poems have appeared in *O.blek, Sulfur, Acts, Notus, Tyuoni, Global City Review, Trafika,* and *apex of the M.* His book *En algún otro lado: México en la poesía de lengua inglesa* (Mexico City: Editorial Vuelta, 1992) is an anthology of twentieth-century poems rendered by North American and British writers— from D. H. Lawrence, Langston Hughes, and William Carlos Williams to Charles Olson and Denise Levertov—engaging Mexico as both cultural reality and imaginative map.

Of "Honeycomb perfection of this form before me . . ." Tejada writes: "There is an increasingly visible rift, throughout the globe, between the individual and his or her link to community or environs. This, in turn, has given rise to a legitimate questioning of how the construct of identity, which is anything but stable, can be doctored by the state, by the powerful industries of information and mass culture, or by timely self-interest. Quite simply, and to the point, 'what we are' is more usefully seen now as inseparable from 'who it is' lending authority to the description, or to the geographically specific, historical 'whereabouts' presumed to be voiced. By asking how it is possible to address one's immediate standing in relation to the weight of the past that brought one here, the series to which this poem belongs is an effort to defend the idea of raising alternative points of representation, multiple voices in contrast to the notion of site as a single body—naming a particular elsewhere whose artifacts would solicit a public dreaming that layered the often-overbearing image of the present."

CHASE TWICHELL was born in New Haven, Connecticut, in 1950. She is the author of four books of poems, most recently *The Ghost of Eden* (Ontario Review Press, 1995). Her earlier books are *Perdido* (Farrar, Straus & Giroux, 1991), *The Odds* (Pittsburgh University Press, 1986), and *Northern Spy* (Pittsburgh, 1981). She is the coeditor with Robin Behn of *The Practice of Poetry: Writing Exercises from Poets Who Teach* (HarperCollins, 1992). She has twice received fellowships from the National Endowment for the Arts (1987, 1993) as well as a Guggenheim Fellowship and an award in literature from the American Academy of Arts and Letters. Currently a lecturer in the creative writing program at Princeton University, she has also taught at Hampshire College and the University of Alabama.

Of "Aisle of Dogs," Twichell writes: "In an animal shelter, I'd seen an abused dog like the pit bull in the poem, but as an image it resisted appropriation. It spoke for itself. What more could a poem do with it? I crumpled a lot of paper trying to answer that question. In the end, 'Aisle of Dogs' says what it saw, and then says it knows that's not enough. That confession becomes its reason for being. As a poem, that's as far as it goes, because that's as far as I could go when I was writing it. In this way, each new poem seems to me a monument to my ignorance. I mean that quite literally. A poem shows the state of the poet's consciousness when he wrote it, like a mosquito in amber. That's why the act of making a poem is both intimate and public, and why it's impossible to learn how to write one—it's always the *next* one that's important, the one still in the dark. It's also why poems—good ones, anyway—are places where one human spirit can come face-to-face with another, flaws and failures of courage included. It's why we read them and why we try to write them."

LUIS ALBERTO URREA was born in Tijuana, Baja California, to an American mother and a Mexican father in 1955. He makes his living as a full-time writer. He worked for several years as a relief worker on the Mexican side of the border, and he taught workshops in expository prose and creative writing at Harvard in the 1980s. He divides his time between the Rockies, the Sonoran Desert, and Mexico City. At the moment he is living in Tucson, researching and writing a long novel about his great aunt, Teresa Urrea, the Saint of Cabora. His books include *Across the Wire* (Anchor Books, 1993), *In Search of Snow* (HarperCollins, 1994), *The Fever of Being* (West End Press, 1994), and *By the Lake of Sleeping Children* (Anchor Books, 1996), a book of essays about the border between the U.S. and Mexico.

Urrea writes: "'Ghost Sickness' is a poem that took me decades to write. In 1970, I was living like a feral child in Culiacan and points south. I had been dragged down there by my father for various reasons, but mostly to 'make me a man.' He left me there and went back to California, and I went off like a roman candle, throwing sparks of my soul all over the tropics. During that summer, I contracted paratyphoid, and I sweltered in the heat and humidity. With a high fever, I hallucinated day and night. Once I watched a parade of Americans walk across the sky in single file. A twenty-seven-hour bus trip home and a stay in isolation in an American hospital ended the summer. I could not distinguish between my actual memories and my fever dreams, which is where this poem sinks its taproot: in the loamy valley in between. I know the whorehouse section is true. I may not have learned anything at all about the alien process of being a man, but I have learned a little about poems."

JEAN VALENTINE was born in Chicago in 1934. She lived and taught for many years in New York City; she now lives in County Sligo, Ireland. Her most recent book is *The River at Wolf* (Alice James Books, 1992); her next book, *Growing Darkness, Growing Light,* will be published by Carnegie Mellon in 1997. Other volumes include *Home, Deep, Blue: New and Selected Poems* (Alice James Books) and *The Messenger* (Farrar Straus & Giroux).

Of "Tell Me, What Is the Soul," Valentine writes, "A swallow flying into a banquet hall and out again, into the night, was an early image of the soul. This description of Mandelstam, when he was last seen, in a transit camp, is another image of the soul, for our time."

ALMA LUZ VILLANUEVA was born in Santa Barbara, California, in 1944, and grew up in San Francisco's Mission District. She is a poet, novelist, short story writer, essayist, and occasional teacher. She is the author of six books of poetry, most recently *Planet* (Bilingual Press, Arizona State University, 1994), which received the 1994 Latin American Writers Institute Award. Her novel *The Ultraviolet Sky* (Bilingual Press, 1988; Doubleday, 1994) won the 1988 American Book Award. Her other books include *Naked Ladies*, winner of the PEN-Oakland fiction award, and *Weeping Woman: La Llorona and Other Stories*, both from Bilingual Press. Her essays have been published in *Ms.* and in anthologies such as *Hot Flashes* (Faber & Faber, 1995).

Of "Crazy Courage," Villanueva writes: "I wrote this poem about a memorable student I had in two classes—one fiction, the other poetry. Michael came to the first class, fiction, as a man, a very brilliant man, struggling to find his voice and vision as a writer. In the next (poetry) class, about a year later, Michael was sitting across from me, but I didn't recognize him.

"At the end of the first class, an interesting-looking, slender woman, very stylishly dressed, came up to speak to me. She said, 'Do you recognize me?' The voice, the eyes. To say I was shocked is an understatement. I was stunned. Michael stood there gently smiling, amused and enjoying my total confusion as I pulled reality together: This is Michael. Then I laughed. And laughed. I stood up and hugged him, and we went out to talk on the grass. I liked him as a man, and I definitely liked him as a woman. In fact, I noticed I was more comfortable with him as a woman. We sat closer, I touched him more. And he felt more comfortable with me. I was amazed by this transformation, and delighted, but I also worried about him. Was he safe 'out there'?

"Michael's presence in our poetry class taught everyone something. Something personal. I don't pretend to know what he taught everyone, but I think it had to do with courage. This poem is my tribute to his crazy courage."

KAREN VOLKMAN was born in Miami in 1967 and educated at New College, Syracuse University, and the University of Houston. Her first book of poems, *Crash's Law,* was a 1995 National Poetry Series selection, chosen by Heather McHugh, and published by W. W. Norton in 1996. Her poems have appeared in *Poetry, The Paris Review, American Poetry Review,* and *Partisan Review.* She received a National Endowment for the Arts Fellowship in Poetry for 1993–94, and has been a resident at the MacDowell Colony and at Yaddo. Currently, she lives in Brooklyn and teaches at New York University.

Volkman writes: "'The Case' is a poem I strongly resisted writing. Only after its odd repetitions had circled in my head for several months did I finally give in and put it down on paper. It seemed so peculiar, airy, and unanchored that I could hardly acknowledge it as a poem at all—more as a supplicating voice in the void. As *Crash's Law* evolved, I came to see the poem as one version of an obsessive motif: the encounter between a nascent, questioning spirit and a destructive, erotic demon (or deity) who responds with brutal and unanswerable force. 'The Case' helped reveal to me that my deepest concern as a poet is an attention to states of consciousness, particularly the spiritual peril and violence that compose the larger part of our waking and dreaming life."

DIANE WAKOSKI was born in Whittier, California, in 1937. She has been writer-in-residence (and *ex officio* 'Moon Lady') at Michigan State University since 1975. She is married to the photographer Robert Turney and is the author of twenty-one collections of poetry. Her most recent book, *The Emerald City of Las Vegas* (Black Sparrow, 1995), joins *Medea the Sorceress* (Black Sparrow, 1991) and *Jason the Sailor* (Black Sparrow, 1993) to form a three-volume epic of the West called *The Archaeology of Movies and Books.*

Of "The Butcher's Apron," Wakoski writes: "In this poem, I try to present my aesthetics and perhaps also a sketchy theory about art. For me, beauty is an obsession. I have always wished my life were more like a work of art. One of my pleasures is attempting to transform images from my life into poems, often with the hope that they might almost seem to be paintings or pieces of music. In 'The Butcher's Apron,' I tried to make a painting out of these images from my life. I give a clue to this by mentioning O'Keefe and Warhol, but I also mention Plath not so much as an allusion to her poetry but to suggest the idea of music, since she represents her hospital-room tulips as objects that make vibrant sound. As a poet, I want to suggest from the butcher metaphor that art is the cutting up of substance, meat, ourselves, so that it can be used to nourish us. But more than that, I want an image of the visceral—blood—as the beginning of painting or poetry or music. I titled my first large collection of poems *Inside the Blood Factory* (Doubleday, 1968), and in that title I also wanted to call attention to the visceral image of blood, our bodies as blood factories, manufacturing the cells of our lives: our bodies as artists or artisans, creators or manufacturers of something vital. I suppose this poem simply carries on that theme."

RON WELBURN was born in Berwyn, Pennsylvania, in 1944 and grew up there and in Philadelphia. He is of Cherokee and Conoy Indian and black descent. He reviews jazz and folk recordings and has written five collections of poetry, including *Council Decisions* (1991). In 1992 he attended the first Returning the Gift Native American Writers Festival, and he is a member of the Wordcraft Circle. He teaches Native American literature at the University of Massachusetts at Amherst.

Of "Yellow Wolf Spirit," he writes: "The opening lines reflect the atmosphere for this special personal experience. I had spent the day as one of Chippewa writer Gerald Vizenor's colleagues in a state Humanities Foundation workshop before driving that night on the Mass Pike to the Chrisjohn family's Oneida powwow. That Indians respect wolves as wise teachers had particular resonance for me, and as the poem aims to impart something of what we learn about our lives, I incorporated popular culture images of machismo and European-based perception of wolves in a way I hope the spirit of the entire poem reverses. I believe 'Yellow Wolf Spirit' is a teaching device, and I read it at the 1993 Phi Beta Kappa ceremonies on campus."

SUSAN WHEELER was born in Pittsburgh in 1955, and grew up in Minnesota, Connecticut, and Massachusetts. She attended Bennington College as an undergraduate in literature and the University of Chicago as a graduate student in art history; there she received the John Billings Fiske Poetry Prize. Her first collection of poetry, *Bag o' Diamonds,* published by the University of Georgia Press in 1993, was chosen by James Tate to receive the Norma Farber First Book Award of the Poetry Society of America in 1994, and was short-listed for the Los Angeles Times Book Award in poetry. Her work has appeared in the 1988, 1991, and 1993 editions of *The Best American Poetry* anthology and in the 1994 *Pushcart Prize.* She regularly contributes essays on French poetry to *The Denver Quarterly,* and was a 1993–95 Fellow of the New York Foundation on the Arts. She teaches creative writing at Rutgers University and at the New School for Social Research in New York

City, where she will serve on the inaugural faculty of the MFA program in creative writing admitting its first degree candidates in the fall of 1996. She lives in New York City with her husband, a scientist.

Of "Run on a Warehouse," Wheeler writes: "Some poems seem to be assembled as a dream is, with elements plucked from life but a structure that seems to come out of nowhere. My husband was skiing in Montana, and we were at that time negotiating together a furniture choice. Once the first stanza surfaced from these banal facts, the rest followed."

PAUL WILLIS was born in Fullerton, California, in 1955. He was raised in Corvallis, Oregon, and educated at Wheaton College and Washington State University. He is an associate professor of English at Westmont College in Santa Barbara, California, where he lives with his wife and two children. He has written a pair of wilderness fantasy novels, *No Clock in the Forest* and *The Stolen River* (Avon, 1993).

Of "Meeting Like This," Willis writes: "This is an unusual effort in that it is written out of someone else's experience. I have never met Dave Foreman, the founder of the environmental group Earth First! that staged a series of road-building blockades in the pristine mountains and forests of southern Oregon in 1983. From my brother Dave Willis, another wilderness activist, I heard the story of how Foreman had been run over by the workers in the pickup truck. Ten years later, my brother wrote me a letter about their rowing adventure in Hell's Canyon, and I thought I would try to juxtapose the two experiences in a poem."

ANNE WINTERS was born in St. Paul in 1939. She is the author of *The Key to the City* (Chicago University Press, 1986), a book of poems nominated for the National Book Critics Circle Prize, and the translator of *Salamander: Selected Poems of Robert Marteau* (Princeton University Press, 1979), which won *Poetry*'s Glatstein Award. Her poems, essays, and translations have appeared in *The Paris Review, The New Yorker, The New Republic, Poetry, The Yale Review,* and elsewhere, and she has been a recipient of an Ingram Merrill Foundation grant and a National Endowment for the Arts Fellowship. She teaches English and comparative literature at Bennington College and is on the core faculty of the Bennington Writing Seminars, the college's low-residency MFA program in creative writing.

Of "The Mill-Race," Winters writes: "When I was about twenty I worked as a typist in an import-export firm on Whitehall Street near the Battery in Manhattan, and recently I went back down there around quitting time. It must be the world's densest concentration of office workers, mainly women, and when they all come down into the streets, ferries, buses, and subways at once, you feel both the force of their numbers, and thousands of signs of individuation that struggle against the deformations of training a life against this work world. Later I was curious about the hundreds of drivers and unmarked cars massed below the skyscrapers; a driver explained they were prepaid by firms to take executives home."

C. DALE YOUNG was born in 1969 and grew up in the Caribbean and south Florida. He received a BS from Boston College in 1991 and, in 1993, an MFA from the University of Florida, where he now attends medical school. He is scheduled to receive the MD in 1997. His poems have appeared in *Antioch Review, Partisan Review, The Southern Review, The Southwest Review, The New Criterion,* and *The Formalist.* He currently holds the position of poetry consultant at the *New England Review.*

Young writes: "'Vespers' holds as its genesis a postcard, a photograph I saw at an exhibit on South America, calligraphy, and something I heard my mother say when I was young. The postcard had young girls washing clothes in a river; the photograph, a woman swinging a man's shirt up into the air. The calligraphy was from my sophomore year in high school. My mother's statement: 'There are few things more sobering than the icy water of a river at sunrise.' The poem began the way many of my poems do, with the realization that two things were related (related in my mind at least). And so when I saw that photograph and noticed how the woman's arms resembled the chancery *f*'s I had learned in calligraphy, I somehow remembered the postcard, and then there was little I could do to stop the poem. It devoured my Catholic-school guilt, the Crusades, rose-apple blossoms, even the word *benediction.* Though this may seem odd to some, I have met several poets in the past few years who also give themselves over to this junk shop method of composition."

RAY A. YOUNG BEAR was born in 1950. He is a poet, novelist, and performing artist. A frequent contributor to the field and study of contemporary Native American literature, he is a tribal member of the Meskwaki Nation of central Iowa. His latest book is a novel, *Remnants of the First Earth,* to be published by Grove/Atlantic Monthly Press in 1996. His books of poetry are *Black Eagle Child* (University of Iowa Press, 1992); *The Invisible Musician* (Holy Cow! Press, 1990); and *Winter of the Salamander* (Harper & Row, 1980). Young Bear has taught at Eastern Washington University, Iowa State University, and the University of Iowa. With his spouse, Stella, he is a drummer and cofounder of the Black Eagle Child Dance Troupe. Under the Woodland Singers title they have recorded traditional songs (Canyon Records, 1987). Young Bear also writes essays and editorials for the *Des Moines Sunday Register.*

Of "Our Bird Aegis," Young Bear writes: "Based on a fictional tribe called Black Eagle Child, this poem was originally intended to depict the plight of an ancient Woodlands people floating on their earth-island amid an ocean of modernity in rural Americana. Yet at the same time—and this is the way I write poems or novels—I was thinking of my father's name: *Ma ka te Ke ti wa,* or Black Eagle. Since my father is a Bear clan leader here on tribally bought land in central Iowa, his name has always been a source of fascination. For whatever reason, I wouldn't ask him for a long time how that particular name came to be. It was surprising to learn that he had not asked the same of his father either. But he did learn that Black Eagle was Bear clan oriented, and with this knowledge came a story. Regrettably, the name-story, for whatever reason, was not imparted by my grandfather.

"In 1973, I became reacquainted with eagle symbolisms through my wife, Stella Lasley, whose Eagle clan name is *Wa se ke kwa,* or the Glint of the Sun on a Turning Eagle's Wing. Interestingly enough, her father's name is *Wa bi Ke ti wa,* or Gray Eagle. In short, there are strong, prevailing influences of nature—bird, fish, animal, weather, and so forth—in our Meskwaki—'People of the Red Earth'—names.

"In the poem I juxtapose the Bear and Eagle clan deities via the young bird viewing its own metamorphic tracks. There is an admixture of bird and animal motifs that sometimes overlap, as well as real or imagined clans, names, and people who live in ordinary and supernatural realities. And from my beloved late grandmother's stories, including references that have been in libraries for the past seventy-five years, the element of snow equals the return of the Creator. In a way, it also signifies the heavy branch-breaking snow that was part of the battle between goodness and evil in our tribal creation stories.

"The word *massive* in the second stanza alludes to my late brother, Todd Dana Young Bear. At first, I wanted to use his earthly name, *Wa ba ko na ka,* or A Bear Scratching a Tree White, but instead I used *Me kwi so ta,* which is a real, all-inclusive Meskwaki term meaning The One Who Is Bear Clan-Named. For this I contemplated my father's important tribal role, something I could never duplicate.

"The fourth stanza shifts back to the fictional tribe, the plight they endure, and their bird symbol. Not only are tribal peoples suffering but the deities themselves become victimized in the process of acculturation. In the last stanza the deity spots the narrator, me, and the situation returns to the personal present: the deity is aware of our family loss. But according to Meskwaki custom, it cannot express its emotions. From childhood we are thus told not to shed tears or mention the names of the deceased. In our anguish there is inner healing, which translates into eternal resolve for those in the 'Grandfather world.' One could say that in spite of everything that has happened to Native Americans over the course of five centuries of cultural malignment and even through today, we remain mindful of the beliefs that were 'given' so long ago."

MAGAZINES WHERE THE POEMS
WERE FIRST PUBLISHED

Alaska Quarterly Review, ed. Ronald Spatz. University of Alaska, 3211 Providence Drive, Anchorage, Alaska 99508.

The American Voice, ed. Frederick Smock. The Kentucky Foundation for Women, Inc., 332 West Broadway, Louisville, Kentucky 40202.

The Americas Review, ed. Lauro H. Flores. University of Houston, Houston, Texas 77204-2090.

Another Chicago Magazine, eds. Lee Webster and Barry Silesky. 3709 North Kenmore, Chicago, Illinois 60613.

The Atlantic Monthly, ed. Peter Davison. 745 Boylston Street, Boston, Massachusetts 02116.

Beloit Poetry Journal, ed. Marion K. Stocking. Box 154, RFD 2, Ellsworth, Maine 04605.

Callaloo, ed. Charles H. Rowell. University of Virginia, Department of English, Wilson Hall, Charlottesville, Virginia 22903.

Colorado Review, poetry ed. Jorie Graham. 359 Eddy/Department of English, Colorado State University, Fort Collins, Colorado 80523.

Cream City Review, ed. Aedan Alexander Hanley. University of Wisconsin, Department of English, P.O. Box 413, Milwaukee, Wisconsin 53201.

Drumvoices Revue, ed. Eugene B. Redmond. Department of English, Box 1431, Southern Illinois University, Edwardsville, Illinois 62026-1431.

Extracts from Pelican Bay: An Anthology of Prisoner Poetry, Drawings, and Essays, ed. Marilla Arguelles. Pelican Bay Information Project, 2489 Mission Street, #28, San Francisco, California 94110.

Farmer's Market, poetry ed. Joanne Lowery. Elgin Community College, 1700 Spartan Drive, Elgin, Illinois 60123-7193.

Field, eds. Stuart Friebert and David Young. Rice Hall, Oberlin College, Oberlin, Ohio 44074.

Fourteen Hills: The San Francisco State University Review, ed. Elsa Dixon. Department of Creative Writing, San Francisco State University, 1600 Holloway Avenue, San Francisco, California 94132-1722.

Hanging Loose, eds. Robert Hershon, Dick Lourie, Mark Pawlak, and Ron Schreiber. 231 Wyckoff Street, Brooklyn, New York 11217.

Indiana Review, ed. Shirley Stephenson. Indiana University, 316 North Jordan, Bloomington, Indiana 47405.

In Time: Women's Poetry from Prison, eds. Rosanna Warren and Teresa Iverson. Boston University, 745 Commonwealth Avenue, Boston, Massachusetts 02215.

The Iowa Review, ed. David Hamilton. 308 EPB, University of Iowa, Iowa City, Iowa 52242-1408.

The Kenyon Review, ed. David H. Lynn. Kenyon College, Gambier, Ohio 43022.

Lingo, ed. Jonathan Gams. P.O. Box 184, West Stockbridge, Massachusetts 01266.

Mānoa, eds. Robert Shapard and Frank Stewart. English Department, University of Hawaii, Honolulu, Hawaii 96822.

Many Mountains Moving, poetry ed. Marilyn Krysl. 420 East 22nd Street, Boulder, Colorado 80302.

The New York Times, op-ed page ed. Mitchell Levitas. 229 West 43rd Street, New York, New York 10036.

The New Yorker, poetry ed. Alice Quinn. 20 West 43rd Street, New York, New York 10036.

No Roses Review, eds. San Juanita Garza, Natalie Kenvin, Carolyn Koo. P.O. Box 597781, Chicago, Illinois 60659.

The North American Review, poetry ed. Peter Cooley. University of Northern Iowa, 1227 West 27th Street, Cedar Falls, Iowa 50614-0516.

The Occident, ed. Brian Malesa. Box 11741, Berkeley, California 94712.

The Paris Review, poetry ed. Richard Howard. 541 East 72nd Street, New York, New York 10021.

Ploughshares, poetry ed. David Daniel. Emerson College, 100 Beacon Street, Boston, Massachusetts 02116.

Poetry, ed. Joseph Parisi. 60 West Walton Street, Chicago, Illinois 60610.

Poetry Flash, ed. Joyce Jenkins, P.O. Box 4172, Berkeley, California 94704. Phone: (415)525-5476.

Poetry Northwest, ed. David Wagoner. University of Washington, 4045 Brooklyn Avenue NE, Seattle, Washington 98195.

Prairie Schooner, ed. Hilda Raz. University of Nebraska, 201 Andrews Hall, Lincoln, Nebraska 68588-0334.

Private, ed. Dale Heiniger. Box 10936, Chicago, Illinois 60610.

The Progressive, ed. Matthew Rothschild, 409 East Main Street, Madison, Wisconsin 53703.

River City, ed. Paul Naylor. Department of English, University of Memphis, Memphis, Tennessee 38152.

River Styx, ed. Lee Fournier. 3207 Washington, St. Louis, Missouri 63103.

The Southern Review, eds. James Olney and Dave Smith. 43 Allen Hall, Louisiana State University, Baton Rouge, Louisiana 70803-5005.

Sulfur, ed. Clayton Eshleman. English Department, Eastern Michigan University, Ypsilanti, Michigan 48197.

The Texas Observer, poetry ed. Naomi Shihab Nye. 307 West 7th Street, Austin, Texas 78701.

TriQuarterly, ed. Reginald Gibbons. Northwestern University, 2020 Ridge Avenue, Evanston, Illinois 60208.

Weber Studies, ed. Neila Seshachari. Weber State University, Ogden, Utah 84408-1214.

ACKNOWLEDGMENTS

The series editor wishes to thank his assistants, Maggie Nelson and C. A. Carlson, for their invaluable help. Thanks, too, go to Glen Hartley and Lynn Chu of Writers' Representatives, Inc.; Beth Gylys of the University of Cincinnati; and Hamilton Cain, Jennifer Chen, Sharon Dynak, and Nan Graham of Scribner.

Grateful acknowledgment is made to the editors of the publications from which the poems in this volume were chosen. Unless specifically noted otherwise, copyright of the poems is held by the individual poets.

Latif Asad Abdullah: "The Tombs" appeared in *Extracts from Pelican Bay*. Reprinted by permission of Marilla Argüelles and The Pelican Bay Information Project.

Sherman Alexie: "Capital Punishment" appeared in *Indiana Review*. Reprinted by permission of the poet.

Margaret Atwood: "Morning in the Burned House" appeared in *The North American Review*. Reprinted by permission of the poet.

Thomas Avena: "Cancer Garden" appeared in *The Occident*. Reprinted by permission of the poet.

Marie Annharte Baker: "Porkskin Panorama" appeared in *Callaloo*. Reprinted by permission of the poet.

Sidney Burris: "Strong's Winter" appeared in *The Southern Review*. Reprinted by permission of the poet.

Rosemary Catacalos: "David Talamántez on the Last Day of Second Grade" appeared in *The Texas Observer*. Reprinted by permission of the poet.

Marilyn Chin: "Cauldron" appeared in *The Kenyon Review*. Reprinted by permission of the poet.

Wanda Coleman: "American Sonnet (35)" appeared in *River City*. Reprinted by permission of the poet.

Jacqueline Dash: "Me Again" appeared in *In Time*. Reprinted by permission of the poet.

Ingrid de Kok: "Transfer" appeared in *TriQuarterly*. Reprinted by permission of the poet.

William Dickey: "The Arrival of the *Titanic*" first appeared in *Poetry*, copyright December 1995 William Dickey. Reprinted by permission of the editor of *Poetry*.

Nancy Eimers: "A History of Navigation" appeared in *Poetry Northwest*. Reprinted by permission of the poet.

Nancy Eimers: "A Night Without Stars" appeared in *Alaska Quarterly Review*. Reprinted by permission of the poet.

Martín Espada: "Sleeping on the Bus" appeared in *The Progressive*. Reprinted by permission of the poet.

Valerie Martínez: "It Is Not" appeared in *Prairie Schooner*. Reprinted by permission of the poet.

Davis McCombs: "The River and Under the River" appeared in *No Roses Review*. Reprinted by permission of the poet.

Sandra McPherson: "Edge Effect" first appeared in *Poetry*, copyright July 1995 Sandra McPherson. Reprinted with the permission of the editor of *Poetry*.

James Merrill: "b o d y" appeared in *The New York Times*. "b o d y" is from *A Scattering of Salts* by James Merrill. Copyright © 1995 by James Merrill. Reprinted by permission of Alfred A. Knopf Inc.

W. S. Merwin: "Lament for the Makers" first appeared in *Poetry*, copyright September 1995 W. S. Merwin. Reprinted by permission of the editor of *Poetry*.

Jane Miller: "Far Away" appeared in *Colorado Review*. Reprinted by permission of the poet.

Susan Mitchell: "Girl Tearing Up Her Face" appeared in *The Paris Review*. Reprinted by permission of the poet.

Pat Mora: "Mangos y limones" appeared in *Prairie Schooner*. Reprinted by permission of the poet.

Alice Notley: "One of the Longest Times" appeared in *Fourteen Hills*. Reprinted by permission of the poet.

Naomi Shihab Nye: "The Small Vases from Hebron" appeared in *Many Mountains Moving*. Reprinted by permission of the poet.

Alicia Ostriker: "The Eighth and Thirteenth" appeared in *Poetry Flash*. Reprinted by permission of the poet.

Raymond Patterson: "Harlem Suite" appeared in *Drumvoices Revue*. Reprinted by permission of the poet.

Carl Phillips: "As from a Quiver of Arrows" appeared in *The Atlantic Monthly*. Reprinted by permission of the poet.

Wang Ping: "Song of Calling Souls" appeared in *Sulfur*. Reprinted by permission of the poet.

Sterling Plumpp: "Two Poems" ["Poet," "When the Spirit Spray Paints the Sky"] appeared in *TriQuarterly*. Reprinted by permission of the poet.

Katherine Alice Power: "Sestina for Jaime" appeared in *In Time*. Reprinted by permission of the poet.

Reynolds Price: "Twenty-One Years" appeared in *The Southern Reivew*. Reprinted by permission of the poet.

Alberto Alvaro Ríos: "Domingo Limón" appeared in *Prairie Schooner*. Reprinted by permission of the poet.

Pattiann Rogers: "Abundance and Satisfaction" appeared in *The Iowa Review*. Reprinted by permission of the poet.

Quentin Rowan: "Prometheus at Coney Island" appeared in *Hanging Loose*. Reprinted by permission of the poet.

David Shapiro: "For the Evening Land" appeared in *Lingo*. Reprinted by permission of the poet.

Angela Shaw: "Crepuscule" first appeared in *Poetry*, copyright March 1995 Angela Shaw. Reprinted by permission of the editor of *Poetry*.

Reginald Shepherd: "Skin Trade" appeared in *Ploughshares*. Reprinted by permission of the poet.

CUMULATIVE SERIES INDEX

The following are the annual listings in alphabetical order of poets and poems reprinted in the first eight editions of *The Best American Poetry*.

1988
Edited and Introduced by John Ashbery

1989
Edited and Introduced by Donald Hall

1990
Edited and Introduced by Jorie Graham

1991
Edited and Introduced by Mark Strand

1992

Edited and Introduced by Charles Simic

1993
Edited and Introduced by Louise Glück

1994
Edited and Introduced by A. R. Ammons

1995
Edited and Introduced by Richard Howard